C... KV-578-095

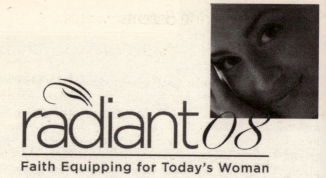

radiant 08

Faith Equipping for Today's Woman

Join an anticipated 1500 women of faith for 4 celebrations, 32 workshops, a pamper room, a fair trade fashion show, late night chick flick and much much more.

Eastbourne Devonshire Park Complex
19th – 21st September 2008

Speakers & Musicians Include:

Lou Fellingham, Ali Herbert, Faith Forster, Catherine Butcher, Sue Prosser, Nia Price, Fiona Castle (TBC), Jennifer Rees Larcombe, Lindsay Melluish, Wendy Virgo, Kelly Minter, Gail Chamberlain, Amy Orr Ewing, Nancy Goudie, Sue Owen, Mo Tizzard, Sharon Anson, Jane Bullivant, Sheila Bridge, Maggie Ellis, Lee Jackson (and more yet to be confirmed)

A Kingsway Trust Project In partnership with
Woman Alive & Day by Day With God

Go to
www.radiantconference.com
for more information

www.womanalive.co.uk
www.daybydaywithgod.com

Catherine Butcher writes...

'Those who look to him are *radiant*; their faces are never covered with shame,' says Psalm 34:5.

Day by Day with God is designed to produce radiant women, but the only makeover we're advocating is the type God does—transforming our lives as we look to him. To encourage that ongoing transformation, *Day by Day with God* is backing *Radiant 08*, a conference for women, which we are promoting together with publisher Kingsway and the Christian women's magazine *Woman Alive*. The event takes place at Eastbourne's Devonshire Park Complex in Sussex from 19 to 21 September 2008, and several *Day by Day with God* contributors will be taking part. See the advert opposite to find out more.

It is my prayer that, as you use these daily devotional readings, your life will be transformed so that you radiate God's love and grace. Ask God to use this army of radiant women in homes and offices, at school gates, shopping, and out and about in communities nationwide. Here's how God has used one reader recently:

One of my roles in our church is to tell stories at our Mother & Toddler group. Our children's ages are 0–5 years so I don't have a captive audience for a long timespan! It's the parents, grandparents and carers that bring the children who are my listeners. Because many of these people have little knowledge of the Bible or our Christian faith, I give a great deal of prayer and thought to my words. Two weeks ago I chose the story of the prodigal son and prayed for God to give me the right words. I opened my DBDWG and the reading was Luke 15:11–32. God knows what the DBDWG writers will write and what the readers will need. His timing is immaculate. I've had no training to do the work I do—I've spent my working life behind shop counters—but God is my strength and the Holy Spirit my helper. Thank you for Day by Day with God*—it's so good to read other women's stories and to be inspired by them…*

JEAN, LOWESTOFT

Do let us know how God works in your life as you use *Day by Day with God*. Write to me at BRF, 15 The Chambers, Vineyard, Abingdon OX14 3FE, England, visit us online at www.brf.org.uk or, if you are attending *Radiant 08*, the women's conference in Eastbourne this September, I look forward to meeting you there.

A family story

A man from Bethlehem in Judah, together with his wife and two sons, went to live for a while in the country of Moab.

Welcome to the book of Ruth! It is one of only two books in the Bible titled with a woman's name (the other is Esther), and this should alert our attention. Of course God has many things to say about and through women throughout the Bible, and nowhere more importantly than through the lips and actions of Jesus, but Ruth is in many ways a story especially for us.

And that is exactly what it is—a story. It's a family story, set in the time of the judges and placed in our Bibles between the strife-ridden national panorama of the book of Judges and the vast sweep of Israel's continuing history through the books of Samuel. It's as if God uses his zoom lens on history and draws us into a personal story to engage our emotions and communicate his heart to us.

A couple of years ago, we went to see a film called *World Trade Centre* with our eldest daughter. The film, telling the story of 9/11, zooms in to look at two families, represented by two fathers who find themselves trapped in the wreckage of the Twin Towers and thrown together for about 24 nail-bitingly terrifying hours. Suddenly we were caught up in something we could relate to, because we began to care what happened to the men and their families.

Coming out of the cinema, we walked home clutching each other's hands, the huge priority of loving each other eclipsing every thought and concern.

The book of Ruth, like that film, reminds us that God cares about us and our families, even though we live in a global village and often feel overloaded with information. We can feel so insignificant, but the truth is that we are very significant to our heavenly Father, who cares for our family… and for you and me.

....

Take a minute or two to thank God for your family, and to thank him that he knows and cares about every member of it, whether they know him or not.

AMC

Overwhelmed with grief

'It is more bitter for me than for you, because the Lord's hand has turned against me!'

In the first few verses of this story, a whole family is devastated when Naomi loses her husband and her two sons in a foreign land, Moab—historically a sworn enemy of Israel. Now, however, she has two Moabite daughters-in-law for whom she feels responsible. What is she to do? Having left her home because of a famine, now she hears that the Lord has come to the aid of his people by providing food for them (v. 6) so she sets off with the girls. But there is an inner struggle going on: how will she provide for these two when she has nothing? The right thing to do is to send them back to their families and pray that each finds another husband in time.

When Ruth and Orpah protest at her solution to their dilemma, her grief suddenly comes tumbling out. She feels that she will never recover her life, whereas her daughters-in-law can start again.

Have you ever felt such anguish at the seeming injustice of your situation, especially compared to the circumstances of others? Many years ago, we lost our third child (our first son) to cot death at nine-and-a-half weeks, also in a foreign country. Colour drained from our lives and souls, and the pain was overwhelming. The wonderful truth in the Bible is that God wants to hear our real feelings. David the songwriter says, 'I am feeble and utterly crushed; I groan in anguish of heart' (Psalm 38:8) and Job, who, like Naomi, suffered the loss of everything, says, 'My pain is not relieved… My spirit is broken' (Job 16:6; 17:1). Not only are we free to cast all our cares on him, but the truth is that 'in all things God works for the good of those who love him' (Romans 8:28).

....

Pour out your real feelings about your life today to the Lord. You can shout and cry, and he will still love you!

AMC

Radical faith

Your people will be my people and your God my God… May the Lord deal with me, be it ever so severely, if anything but death separates you and me.

Ruth's famous declaration of faith and commitment is both scary and challenging. She chooses a destiny opposite to Orpah's. She renounces her ethnic and religious roots and opts for a completely unknown, unsecured future. Her leap of faith outdoes even Abraham's in the sense that she acts with no promise in hand, no divine blessing pronounced, no spouse, possessions or supporting community. She gives up the possibility of marriage with one of her own people to devote herself to an ageing woman.

We can't blame Orpah for her choice. She leaves the story here; there are times when people leave our story, but it doesn't mean they don't have their own. Her decision simply highlights Ruth's extraordinary conduct. Orpah did the sensible, expected thing. Ruth did the extraordinary and unexpected. The risk she took foreshadows Jesus' teaching that to be his disciple we must lose our life, in the sense of giving it up to him.

What about us? We probably can't make this 'out of the box' sort of decision, but is there any way, however small, that we could renew our commitment? Could we live without something for a while? I once did a 'clothes fast' for a year, and the truth is that it was exhilarating and led to lots of interesting conversations. Funnily enough, I didn't run out of clothes. I didn't miss shopping, either, but found the experience very liberating. Or perhaps we could decide to fast from food once a week, or to go out of our way to do something kind for someone.

....

Lord, renew a deep, radical faith in me, whatever it takes.

AMC

A chance encounter?

As it turned out, she found herself working in a field belonging to Boaz, who was from the clan of Elimelek.

Well, fancy that! However desperate our circumstances may appear, God is sovereign over our lives, and he often allows us to walk through testing times to forge our character. James says that we should consider trials a 'joy' because they develop our perseverance (James 1:2–3) and Peter says (in the context of being persecuted for our faith) that trials help us to understand the suffering undergone by Jesus (1 Peter 4:13).

Having arrived in Bethlehem as the barley harvest is beginning, Ruth takes action. Firstly, she doesn't wait for Naomi, or the God in whom she now trusts, to bail her out. The principle of cooperating with God is such an important one that we sometimes forget—he expects us to use our common sense. I love Ruth's humility, yet her boldness. She goes and gets a job, and she's not picky. She's not 'too good' for anything. The gleanings were the bits of grain that dropped as the sheaves were being rolled into bundles, and Levitical law stated that they must be left for the poor to gather. Secondly, she is brave: she is obviously a foreigner, and she risks encountering racial tension, since Israel and Moab were sworn enemies. Thirdly, the foreman's report tells us that she is a hard worker.

Enter Boaz, and our romantic nerve endings are tingling! He has presence, is attentive to his workers, immediately notices the new person, and is kind and protective towards her. I wonder if we are people-centred like Boaz. As soon as you decide to make people, not things or plans, your priority, you'll be amazed at what happens. Recently we got into conversation with a Hungarian woman and quickly found out that she was 'with Dawkins' (Richard Dawkins, author of *The God Delusion*). But really she was looking for love, and was clearly touched that we responded to her.

....

Lord, make me people-centred and give me the courage for your God-encounters.

AMC

Under his wings

'May the Lord repay you for what you have done. May you be richly rewarded by the Lord… under whose wings you have come to take refuge.'

In the back of my Bible I have taped a list of 'ouch factor' questions, such as, 'Am I defeated in any part of my life, jealous, impure, critical, irritable, touchy or distrustful?' They were written by the devotional writer, Alan Redpath. Despite the growing equality of men and women in the workplace, many women find themselves taking a back seat in various areas of life, their contributions unseen and unrewarded. And don't we wish someone would laud our efforts? But the truth is that nothing goes unseen, and God is watching our every move.

Here Ruth is most definitely taking a back seat. Life has treated her harshly and we mustn't forget that she is going through bereavement and culture shock—but, as Jesus will exhort his listeners hundreds of years later, she lets her light shine before others and they see her good deeds (Matthew 5:16). She has great integrity.

The blessing that Boaz pronounces over Ruth is rich with dramatic irony, of course, since he himself will be the answer to the prayer within it. He recognizes the cost of what Ruth has done, and that only God can pay the debt of her service. He knows, too, that God is not only a rewarder but a refuge. This reminds us of Psalm 91: 'Whoever dwells in the shelter of the Most High will rest in the shadow of the Almighty… He will cover you with his feathers, and under his wings you will find refuge' (vv. 1, 4).

When our son Samuel died, these words brought such comfort to us, despite the agony. Truth is so much bigger than time and, if we take refuge in God, things will work out in time.

....

Father, help me to hold integrity close and to wait for your timing. Teach me to seek only for your recognition.

AMC

Sweet relief

Naomi said to her daughter-in-law, 'Why, God bless that man! God hasn't quite walked out on us after all! He still loves us, in bad times as well as good!'

This book could have been called 'Naomi', since it gives us equal insight into the older woman. Particularly, if we look carefully, we see her brokenness, revealed in her saying to the townspeople, 'Call me Mara [meaning bitter], because the Almighty has made my life very bitter. I went away full, but the Lord has brought me back empty' (1:20–21). Perhaps surprisingly, she leaves the initiative to Ruth once they are back in Bethlehem, but this speaks of her deep bereavement and loss, and consequent exhaustion. She has lost everything, including the care of God, it seems.

What a turnaround now! Boaz, explains Naomi, is a relative of Elimelek's. The main responsibilities of a 'kinsman-redeemer' were to restore ownership of family property through 'redemption', or buying back, and to free relatives from poverty-induced slavery, to which Naomi and Ruth were vulnerable in their destitute state. When Ruth gets home after her first day at work, we can hear the relief in Naomi's voice. She had certainly feared for Ruth's personal safety, and perhaps fretted her way through the day.

I can remember the relief flooding through me one bright December day some years ago, when a neurologist pronounced me a 'healthy young woman'. I had suffered three severe epileptic fits when we lived in France and wondered what lay ahead. Like Naomi, I was exhausted, and the road had been hard and discouraging for a while. I'll never forget the physical sense of God's presence as I stood in the sunshine on the steps of the surgery, surveying a beautiful London square. So often, we draw conclusions born out of the temporal—but we are eternal, and we should have timescales that reflect this fact.

Why don't you lay out your current circumstances before God now (even though he knows every word before it's on your tongue: Psalm 139:4). Tell him that you will trust him to bring relief at the perfect moment.

AMC

A daring plan

Ruth said, 'If you say so, I'll do it, just as you've told me.'

We live in a day when mutual suspicion between generations is growing, fuelled by the rapid evolution of cultural mores and the explosion of technology that has left many older people confused and intimidated. People no longer look to their elders for wise advice. Many of us are more like Solomon's son, Rehoboam, who 'rejected the advice the elders gave him and consulted the young men who had grown up with him' (1 Kings 12:8, TNIV). We think that those who are older don't really understand our world. Inter-enerational trust and respect is, in large measure, lost today, and we should pray for its restoration.

We learn something more of Ruth's character here as she agrees to do whatever Naomi says. I shouldn't think many of us would respond like this to a mother-in-law! In addition, Naomi's proposal initially looks like a good old seduction scene. In the threshing season, it was customary for the landowner and his men to spend the night near the threshing floor to protect his grain, so it was a place for male camaraderie and revelry, which inevitably led to illicit sexual encounters.

But hope has energized Naomi, and now she takes the initiative, even though it seems perplexing at first. Naomi's instructions to Ruth to prepare herself to go down to the threshing floor recall the words of Ezekiel 16:9–12, which describe a bride preparing herself. Throughout the Bible, the threshing floor is symbolic of a significant encounter with God—for revelation, for mourning, for repentance, for judgment, for testing, or for coming to terms with something. Of course, the very nature of threshing is to separate the good from the bad, the straw from the grain.

So what will happen here?

Take a few moments to reflect on the intergenerational relationships in your family. Lord, help me to be a peacemaker in my family, and to foster friendship and trust between the generations.

AMC

A dramatic proposition

'Everybody in town knows what a courageous woman you are—a real prize!'

Boaz obviously wasn't very sensitive to perfume, as he fell sound asleep after a riotous evening with his men! But of course he was startled to find a young woman at his feet when he turned over. In the dark, he can't make out who it is, and when he asks, Ruth boldly makes a proposition of marriage: 'I am Ruth your maiden; take me under your protecting wing. You're my close relative, you know… you do have the right to marry me' (v. 9). I'm sure she had the courage to do this because of her confidence and trust in Naomi.

The context of their first private encounter must have been testing. So many such encounters lead to sexual engagement, and, so often, behavioural, mental and health patterns are passed from one generation to another. 'Our ancestors are in our genes, in our bones, in our marrow, in our physiological and emotional make-up. We, in turn, will be written into the children who come after us,' writes Catherine Marshall. But one of the things God shows us here is that even if there are stories of sickness, betrayal or addiction in our family line, they don't have to play out in our lives. Both Ruth and Boaz were descended from ancestors who had acted immorally and broken God's covenant law. (Genesis 38 tells the story of Boaz' forebears, Judah and Tamar, and Genesis 19 recounts the story of Lot, the ancestor of the Moabites.) Generations later, Boaz and Ruth face temptation, as we all do at some time and in some way, but their integrity and covenant commitment to Yahweh give them moral courage.

We can't change our past but, because of our decisions, we can change our future. This story gives us such hope when we face failure or struggle with behaviour patterns.

....

Read the stories of Lot and Judah, and ponder them. Let God's Spirit speak to you through them. Ask God to make you courageous when facing choices.

AMC

God meets our needs

'Bring me the shawl you are wearing and hold it out.'

This story is teaching us that God carries out his work through believers who seize unexpected opportunities as gifts from God.

I don't suppose many of us have had or will have a chance to find a husband in this amazing way! But this story is about involvement in something much bigger than just finding a husband, as we shall see. It's about obedience and courage. It's also about character, and we can learn much from Boaz' treatment of Ruth.

Boaz shows himself to be respectful, protective, generous and honourable—this last in deferring to the closer relative than himself and showing that he is willing to give Ruth up in the interests of integrity. He is also a type of Christ. He offers her water to drink when she is thirsty, reminding us of Jesus' call: 'Let anyone who is thirsty come to me and drink. Whoever believes in me… rivers of living water will flow from within them' (John 7:37–38). He offers her bread and wine when she is out at work, and he is exceedingly generous to her. In today's passage, he gives her far more than she deserves or could earn as he heaps barley into her shawl. Earlier, Naomi had said, 'God has brought me back [to Bethlehem] with nothing but the clothes on my back' (1:21, *THE MESSAGE*).

Provision comes when we least expect it as we trust our heavenly Father. I'll never forget returning a family car to the people who had kindly lent it to us. After a lovely meal, it was time to go, and my husband laid the keys on the table as we thanked our friends profusely. Suddenly the man pushed the keys back across the table and said, 'It's your car now; we've prayed about this and are quite sure!' So often, provision exceeds our expectations. God is 'able to do immeasurably more than all we ask or imagine' (Ephesians 3:20, TNIV).

***

Lord, increase my faith, and help me to know that you will provide at exactly your right moment, even if it's not mine.

AMC

Redemption

'You realize, don't you, that when you buy the field from Naomi, you also get Ruth the Moabite, the widow of our dead relative, along with the redeemer responsibility to have children with her to carry on the family inheritance.'

This scene takes place at the town gate, the equivalent of the town hall in ancient Israel. It was spacious, like a modern town square, and was the normal place for business transactions. Witnesses were readily available since everyone had to pass through on their way to the fields, the threshing floor or other destinations.

The relative who had first right to Naomi's land and to Ruth declines the offer because it would jeopardize his own family's inheritance (v. 6). There is no blame attached to his refusal; it simply highlights Boaz' actions as extraordinary, since presumably such an action would jeopardize his family in exactly the same way. It highlights Boaz' kindness and generosity to the two widows, just as Orpah's decision at the beginning of the story highlights Ruth's kindness to Naomi.

Both Ruth and Boaz are risk-takers, and the source of their risk-taking is love and compassion. I wonder whether you are a risk-taker, preferring to trust God for your resources, or whether you prefer to organize your own provision. Of course we are to be responsible, and to recognize our limitations is a mark of maturity, but letting compassion and generosity guide one's actions is exhilarating—because it means following Christ, who took the greatest risk of all time in redeeming humanity. After all, there was never any guarantee that those redeemed would accept the redemptive act of Jesus' death on the cross.

What happens to Ruth here is just what happens when we give ourselves to Christ. Metaphorically, we take off our sandal and give it to him. We say, 'I relinquish control over my life; I am yours from this moment on.'

....

Have you lost the exhilaration of your early days as a follower of Jesus? Do you fear handing over control to him? Tell God how you feel.

AMC

15

The power of blessing

'May the Lord make the woman who is coming into your home like Rachel and Leah.'

The Israelite readers of this story would have associated the house of Jacob (Israel), built up by Rachel and Leah, with the house of Israel (the nation), rebuilt after turbulent times by David, the great-grandson of none other than Ruth and Boaz. Here the town dignitaries pray that God will give Ruth the fertility of Rachel and Leah—in other words, that she will have many distinguished children.

To speak here of these famous founding mothers of the nation of Israel is to imply that something much larger is afoot than the birth of one child. There's a hint, through the prayer that Boaz will become famous, that the children born to Boaz and Ruth will be important. Implicit here, also, is the prayer that he will become prosperous through the birth of many children. Today that's a strange idea, as more children usually mean less wealth, but in the agricultural society of their time, more children meant more means of production.

Reading between the lines, chapter 1 suggests that Ruth had suffered infertility: she was married for ten years with no children (vv. 4–5). Today, infertility is increasing and causes many women great anguish of spirit. Perhaps you know someone wrestling with this issue, or going through the emotionally demanding process of IVF. Perhaps you yourself have been crying out to God for some time over this very question. Be encouraged by the turnaround in this story: God hadn't abandoned Ruth, and he won't abandon you or those you love and pray for.

Every year I receive one or two ecstatic letters from people for whom I have prayed that God would give them the child they long for. In our technological age, it's good to remember that ultimately God is the creator of human life (Psalm 139:13), although medical advance brings help to many.

....

Father, raise my faith through the story of Ruth. Give me boldness to pray for children, and constantly remind me that, with you, nothing is impossible.

AMC

Good news at God's chosen time

The women living there said, 'Naomi has a son!' And they named him Obed. He was the father of Jesse, the father of David.

Continuing with yesterday's theme, we must note that 'the Lord enabled [Ruth] to conceive' (v. 13). Not only is this short sentence incredibly faith-building, but it's as if it's a direct answer to the blessing prayer of the previous verses. When we are faced with a faith challenge of these dimensions, we need to remind ourselves that all life proceeds from God.

Ruth's is such a community-centred story. Everyone is overjoyed and excited by the birth of Obed—not just the immediate family of Boaz, Ruth and Naomi, but all the women who are Naomi's friends. We might speculate that Boaz' other dependants were glad too—but today family communities are often scattered round the globe, or scattered through the breakdown of relationship or the fear of commitment.

We can take heart from this wonderful story and pray for God's intervention in the lives of our relatives and friends. Perhaps you need him to intervene in your own life? He is longing to do so: Isaiah 30:18 says that he 'longs to be gracious to you… he will rise up to show you compassion. Be inspired by Ruth's courage and determination, and Naomi's steadfast perseverance and patience. Whether you feel that life has passed you by and you've missed what you aspired to, or you are a young person struggling with feelings of failure in a tough world, it is never too early or too late for God to intervene and transform you and your circumstances.

Good news is so invigorating and regenerating for everyone. When our son Jack was born on a Sunday (17 months after Samuel had died) and my husband, a young curate at the time, went straight to church from the hospital, the people burst out crying and clapping at the same time.

....

Take a moment to recall a moment of really wonderful news, then thank God for it. 'The Lord has done great things for us, and we are filled with joy.'

AMC

17

The big picture

**Judah the father of Perez and Zerah, whose mother was Tamar…
Salmon the father of Boaz, whose mother was Rahab, Boaz the
father of Obed, whose mother was Ruth, Obed the father of Jesse,
and Jesse the father of King David.**

Perez and his twin brother Zerah were the offspring of the union of
Judah with his daughter-in-law Tamar through trickery and deceit
(Genesis 38); in other words, he was the child of his mother and
grandfather. Like Ruth, Tamar was a foreigner who perpetuated a
family line threatened with extinction, but which later became very
prominent in the tribe of Judah. And all this happened through the
mercy of God. So both Tamar and Ruth became famous as founding
mothers. Indeed, both of them are named in Matthew's genealogy of
Jesus, two of only four women named in a very long list.

So often, we feel that we have messed up irretrievably. We see as
the world sees and not as humanity's loving Father in heaven sees: if
you are 'successful' in some way as the world defines the word, you
count. But this wonderful story demonstrates God's gracious and pre-
cise care for two defenceless widows, which results in mended lives
that affect the history of a nation through their descendants. Isn't that
a revolutionary message, both for us and anyone we can tell?

Many people we read about are born in humble circumstances
but rise to make a mark of some kind in their time. Perhaps one of
the most famous examples was Mother Teresa, but you could be one
of them. There is an instinctive longing to count, which is written into
the DNA of humankind. 'He has… set eternity in the human heart'
(Ecclesiastes 3:11, TNIV).

The book of Ruth makes it possible for each of us, however ordinary, to see ourselves as irreplaceable in the telling of God's story.
We do count—every last one of us—and what we do counts.

....

*Lord, thank you that my life fits into your eternal scheme. Teach me
how to connect with your plan.*

AMC

Anita Cleverly writes: 'In 2006, on a trip to Israel, I stood in the fields of Boaz, feeling the power of history beneath my feet. Our guide was an archaeologist, and his understanding of the ground released our understanding of different events as he explained the history and stones.

'Meditation is a bit like archaeology; the deeper you dig, the more you piece together things you didn't initially understand. You dig elsewhere to complement the emerging picture of the site you're on. It can be a long, hot business. Our friend said, "It's amazing that today young people pay thousands of pounds and fly hundreds of miles to join a dig under a boiling sun for a month or so, then go home and tell everyone they've had a fabulous time."

'Meditation should be like that. The trouble is, most of us don't know what we're missing. We are unaware that we're biblically starving. Twenty years ago, our youngest daughter, then 18 months old, was very sick on a flight to America and became dehydrated. Only an unnatural lethargy alerted us to call the paramedics, who whisked her into hospital and on to a life-saving drip. She'd been in danger but refusing nourishment. Many of us are biblically dehydrated but unaware of it.

'Meditation is about knowing rather than knowing about; it's like eating the food rather than looking at the contents of your larder and knowing exactly what you've got in great detail. To meditate is to chew over the word, much as a cow chews over the cud, extracting every drop of goodness. Someone has said that if you know how to worry, you know how to meditate! So that probably includes you!'

As you look into God's word each day, dig deep. Ask the Lord to draw you into the depths of his word, to give you a new passion to understand his heart, taking away any lethargy and filling you with hunger for the bread of life.

Having looked at Ruth's life over the past two weeks, be encouraged by the way God intervened in the life of one widowed immigrant with fertility problems. Her life played a crucial part in Jewish history and she is listed as one of Jesus' forebears. Over the next two weeks, Fiona Barnard will be pointing us to some less prominent characters. Take further encouragement from God's dealings with these rough diamonds and hidden gems.

Naming sorrows

The Lord knew that Jacob loved Rachel more than he did Leah, and so he gave children to Leah, but not to Rachel. Leah gave birth to a son and named him Reuben, because she said, 'The Lord has taken away my sorrow. Now my husband will love me more than he does Rachel.'

'What can I do to make him love me? If only he could see we are made for each other!' The anguish of unrequited love, or of a love gone dead, is unlike any other. Where can you go with all that heartache?

For Leah, a lifetime's pain over being less attractive than her sister was intensified when it became obvious that the husband they shared treated Rachel as his favourite. Leah never stood a chance, playing second fiddle once again in this new household.

However, if love was a luxury in those days, a wife might make her husband happy by producing babies—and here, Leah excelled. What is so moving is the way in which each child's name reflects Leah's trust in a God who understood her suffering. Reuben represented her hope that she might yet be valued by Jacob. Simeon was so called because 'The Lord has heard that my husband doesn't love me.' Levi continued the theme: 'Now my husband will hold me close.' When Judah was given, her response was, 'I'll praise the Lord!'

Amid all the unhappiness and jealousy, scheming and ill-feeling that this tale describes, God is present. Even in the ugly scenes, we see God's unfolding purposes in creating a great nation, the twelve tribes of Israel, from Jacob's twelve sons.

Our relationships may leave us wounded and bemused; our hearts may break; and yet it may not all be wasted if we can seek God in the mess. There is hope if we can trust God to create new life that has his name on it.

....

Place your sorrows before God, and ask for his intervention in the nitty-gritty of your life.

Reading Psalm 57 may give voice to your prayer.

FB

Following wholeheartedly

'Here I am today, eighty-five years old! I am still as strong today as the day Moses sent me out; I'm just as vigorous to go out to battle now as I was then. Now give me this hill country that the Lord promised me that day.'

When I worked as a pastoral assistant, my flatmate could sometimes guess who I had been visiting that day. 'Was it Nan?' she'd ask if I returned grumpy, or 'Was it Mary?' if I came back energized.

Mary had been a missionary in Chile. She loved the country, its people and culture and language. She was full of stories of how God had provided for her in impossible situations. She didn't gloss over painful experiences but what radiated from her was a love for Christ and a commitment to continue serving him, despite debilitating ill health. It made me want to be and do the same.

Caleb, too, followed the Lord wholeheartedly when, as one of twelve, he went to spy out the land that God had promised his people. Ten of his colleagues reported impossible obstacles when they returned, and paralysed everyone into terrified inaction. Caleb and Joshua were outnumbered and ignored when they urged the people to have faith in what God could do through them.

After half a lifetime, it would have been easy to lose heart. Yet, despite the refusal of the people to trust God for victory, despite 45 years of disappointing wilderness wandering, and despite advancing age, Caleb's faith and resolve were undiminished. He did not waste energy bemoaning the past or the punishment he'd shared with God's faithless people. Forward-looking, he was eager to accomplish more for God. He wanted to claim the land that God had promised; he was ready to complete this unfinished task.

What was this old man's secret? It lies in the closest we get to his epitaph: 'he followed the Lord wholeheartedly' (v. 9).

....

How is God challenging you these days? Pray for the whole-heartedness, perseverance and trust of Caleb. Then, go for it!

For encouragement to persevere, read Hebrews 12:1–3.

FB

21

Turning pain to gain

His mother had named him Jabez, saying, 'I gave birth to him in pain.' Jabez cried out to the God of Israel, 'Oh, that you would bless me... Let your hand be with me, and keep me from harm so that I will be free from pain.' And God granted his request.

Sometimes it is hard to move on. The past casts a chilling shadow on the present. It seems as though you will never be free of painful memories, regrets and disappointments. They are always there, like stalkers.

Jabez didn't have too good a start in life. Born in a culture where names are hugely significant, his mother gave him a name sounding like 'pain'. The circumstances surrounding his birth caused her distress—whether physical or emotional—and she transferred her anguish on to him. And he was never allowed to forget it. Every time someone called him 'Pain!' they reinforced the hurt.

What is notable about Jabez is that he didn't change his name and pretend there was no problem. Nor did he resign himself to his fate and shrivel up, blaming the past for all his present misfortunes. Instead, he faced up to the issues and threw himself on to God. He turned the pain and shame into prayer. He begged God to undo the curse and show him favour. He expressed the longing that, rather than retreat because of difficulties, he might be able to rise to challenges. He asked for God's presence and strength. He requested safety and peace and freedom.

Your painful past experiences will always be part of who you are, but they may also be the means by which you come to experience the height and depth of Jesus' love. As you acknowledge them before him, you may see them in a new perspective. They may be the ways that enable you to experience, in a very special way, God's strength in your weakness.

....

How can your painful experiences be the means of experiencing God's strength?

Read 2 Corinthians 12:1–10 to see how Paul could 'delight in weakness'.

FB

Being loved

God spoke to Hosea... 'Find a whore and marry her. Make this whore the mother of your children. And here's why: This whole country has become a whorehouse, unfaithful to me, God.' Hosea did it. He picked Gomer.

'I want to be loved just for being me, not because of how I look, or how clever or funny I am.' We all cry for unconditional love, yet paradoxically we can also find it hard to accept. It doesn't make sense.

Why did Gomer choose prostitution? Or did she feel there was no choice? What were her feelings and motives? Did she marry Hosea because she loved him or were there other reasons? Why, despite marriage and three children, did she return to other men and have to be bought back by Hosea for the price of a slave? Did she finally find contentment? There are so many questions I would love to ask her!

However, there is one thing that touches me about the mysterious Gomer. When God wanted to demonstrate his unconditional, generous love towards his people, he selected Gomer. When he wished to show that he would keep on wooing them, Gomer was his living visual aid. When he chose to express a love that went beyond transient, shallow feeling, Gomer was the object of that indescribable forgiving and restoring love. And this all took place through Hosea, God's prophet.

If you wonder whether God could possibly love you, consider Gomer. If you think you have sinned too much to be restored, look at Gomer. If you lose patience with yourself for getting things wrong again and again, remember Gomer. If you despair that you will ever be worthy of love, think of Gomer.

She was loved unreservedly, in spite of what she had done. The love Hosea had for her is not even a fraction of the love God has for you. Accept it—allow yourself to be loved.

....

Take time now to receive Jesus' love. Pray for help to enter more deeply into Christ's love, in the words of Ephesians 3:14–21.

FB

23

Speaking God's word

Hilkiah [the high priest]... went to talk with Huldah the prophet... She said: You were sent here by King Josiah, and this is what the Lord God of Israel says to him: 'Josiah, I am the Lord! And I intend to punish this country and everyone in it, just as this book says.'

He looked me square in the eyes and spat out his words like daggers: 'You have the gift of teaching, but you are *not* to use it on men.' He seemed to resent my having any gift at all, and would rather it was exercised on no one. I felt wounded, and then strangely rescued as I remembered Huldah. I had read about her that very morning.

Huldah spoke God's word when King Josiah desperately needed it. She was the one whom the temple staff sought when the discovery of the Book of the Law in the temple brought Josiah to a crisis. The prophets Jeremiah and Zephaniah were also active at this time, but it was this woman who confirmed that the people's unfaithfulness to God would indeed have consequences, as the book stated.

Huldah understood the Lord's word. She knew that God had every right to punish his sinful people. She also communicated God's mercy to Josiah, who expressed great sadness at the nation's betrayal of its covenant promises. She assured him that his prayers had been heard.

Having expounded what God had said in the Book of the Law (probably Deuteronomy), and applied it to the present situation, Huldah disappears from the pages of scripture. Yet for me, 26 centuries later, she appeared again to assure me that God may indeed choose to teach his word to both sexes through a woman. I am not to seek prominence but to get on with the business of knowing him, so that, at the right time, he might use even me to guide people in his ways.

....

How might God be asking you to speak his word to someone today?

Read 2 Corinthians 4:5–7 to remind you how God uses you.

FB

Explaining the meaning

The Levites… went among the people, explaining the meaning of what Ezra had read… The Levites encouraged the people… When the people returned to their homes, they celebrated by eating and drinking and by sharing their food with those in need, because they had understood what had been read to them.

'You read the Bible?' Don looked startled. 'Have you read it today?' he enquired, as though he still couldn't quite believe it. I felt as though I was having to defend my sanity as well as my Christian practice. Don, like many today, sees the Bible as an outdated document of weird stories and bemusing laws. Its language and world are deemed inaccessible, interesting only to ivory-tower academics and eccentrics.

For the disappointed Jewish people who had returned from exile in Babylon, their Hebrew Bible, the Law of Moses, meant little to them. The disruptive events in which their great-great-grandparents had been seized from their homeland and taken far from the centre of worship meant that they had lost touch with their identity as God's people. Ezra realized that they needed to hear the scriptures. They had to know their past so that they could form their future according to God's word. However, the scriptures were in Hebrew and the people were more familiar with Aramaic, the language of the Persian empire.

So Jeshua, Bani, Sherebiah, Jamin, Akkub, Shabbethai, Hodiah, Maaseiah, Kelita, Azariah, Jozabad, Hanan and Pelaiah made a massive contribution. As Ezra read the scriptures aloud, these Levites were scattered among the crowd to explain the words and ideas. They comforted the people and encouraged them to understand and experience the joy that comes from following God. Today, the people with whom we live and work need to know that the Bible is utterly relevant. As we rub shoulders with them, we are the best bridges to bring God's word alive to them. Why? Because it has come alive to us.

....

How can I be a bridge between the Bible and the lives of my family and friends and colleagues today?

Celebrate the wonder of God's word by praying Psalm 19.

FB

Serving humbly

Two men were suggested: one of them was … Justus, and the other was Matthias. Then they all prayed, 'Lord, you know what everyone is like! Show us the one you have chosen to be an apostle and to serve in place of Judas…' They drew names, and Matthias was chosen.

'The job is just right for you. You've got all the qualifications,' they said. They encouraged you to go for it. You spent time considering it and were prepared to make the necessary sacrifices. And then the job was given to someone else. You keep asking yourself, 'What was all that about?'

Justus hadn't been looking for a position. He wasn't a pushy person. And yet, it is the *lack* of information about him that may give us a clue to his character. He had been a disciple from the beginning. He had seen Jesus being baptized and had followed him through gruelling days of travel and preaching and healing. He had heard the stories, witnessed the miracles and watched God's love in action. He had been there when Jesus was killed and had met him alive again. With the others, he received the commission to preach Christ 'in all the world' as Jesus returned to heaven.

Isn't it strange that such a loyal follower and friend is not mentioned in the Gospels? Isn't it odd that someone so close to Jesus is never given recognition for what he did and said? And when, finally, he was acknowledged as eminently suited to become an apostle, how did Justus feel when Matthias was chosen instead? Was he upset or relieved?

True followers of Jesus are focused on him and his honour. Personal gain and power are insignificant. Their service is costly, but they love Jesus so much that they embrace the sacrifice. In disappointment and incomprehension, they identify even more with Christ, and they persevere. I think Justus shows every sign of being just like that.

....

Whose 'Well done!' do you need to hear today?

To remind you of what true discipleship means, read Mark 10:35–45.

FB

Believing alone

When she recognized his voice—Peter's voice!—she was so excited and eager to tell everyone Peter was there that she forgot to open the door and left him standing in the street. But they wouldn't believe her... 'You're crazy,' they said. She stuck by her story, insisting.

When they give you the dignity of listening to you, it doesn't feel as humiliating as being ignored altogether. If you are feeling strong at the time, you protest at being patronized but, if you are less confident, you may start to believe that you have nothing to contribute.

The early believers were in earnest prayer. Christians were being killed for their faith. Peter was in prison and awaiting trial. All they could do was to plead to God for him. Then God answered, and everyone was surprised—Peter himself, as he was led out of jail by an angel, the believers who were praying for him, and the prison soldiers who discovered him gone in the morning.

Yet there was one person who did believe that God had done a miracle—a servant named Rhoda. She didn't even need to see Peter; she believed as soon as she heard his voice on the other side of the door. She was overjoyed that God had answered their prayer. In fact, in her eagerness to break the news, she forgot to let him in. Even when she was ignored and dismissed as being out of her mind, she would not be put off. She kept insisting that it was indeed the one for whom they were praying.

We can smile at this comical story, and yet Rhoda should be remembered not only because she forgot to open the door. She believed immediately. She believed when no one else did. She believed when people called her mad. She persisted in believing even when she was outnumbered and dismissed and humiliated. And she was vindicated.

....

Are you the only believer in your situation? Be encouraged by Rhoda. She was in a minority of one, but she was right!

Paul also had to defend his faith alone: read his amazing reaction in 2 Timothy 4:16–18.

FB

27

Daring to trust

The Lord said to him: 'Get up and go to the house of Judas… When you get there, you will find a man named Saul… Saul is praying, and he has seen a vision. He saw a man named Ananias coming to him.'

Sometimes it seems as though God doesn't have a clue what he is asking. 'Lord, you can't really mean me to do this, can you?' we question. 'Surely you must realize that this is impossible. It is so impractical and messy. It will backfire. You are kidding, aren't you?'

So we can sympathize with Ananias when God spoke to him. At first, he was probably excited that God had chosen him: 'Lord, here I am,' he replied—until he heard what was required. Then he was flabbergasted. Rather than warning him to hide from the notorious Jesus-hater, God was asking Ananias to seek him out. Instead of bringing words of comfort to the persecuted believers, he was telling Ananias to bring healing to a man who had arrived in town to kill them.

Ananias may have wondered if he was hearing correctly when God insisted that this very man had been chosen to preach Christ and suffer for him. Despite his fear, however, he obeyed. He called Saul 'brother'. He placed his hands on Saul in Jesus' name. Saul was healed and filled with the Holy Spirit, and became the apostle Paul, a giant in the early Church and in our New Testament.

But where would Paul have been without Ananias? On the surface, all he did was lay hands on Paul and pray. Yet Ananias also befriended him when most Christians would have been suspicious. He was the human means by which Paul received Jesus' power and commission. He introduced Paul to fellow believers; he demonstrated costly obedience. Actually, it wasn't God who didn't know what he was doing; it was Ananias who didn't have a clue how vital he was in God's amazing plan.

....

Is there someone new to your church whom you can befriend and encourage?

For practical hints about encouraging others, read 1 Thessalonians 5:12–24.

FB

Taking a second chance

Paul said to Barnabas, 'Let's go back and visit the Lord's followers in the cities where we preached...' Barnabas wanted to take along John, whose other name was Mark. But Paul did not want to, because Mark had left them in Pamphylia... Paul and Barnabas argued, then each of them went his own way.

The Myers Briggs Personality Indicator distinguishes between 'judgers', who like to be organized, working to complete projects, and 'perceivers', who like to be flexible and open to change as more information is collected. I am still unsure which I am!

I suspect that Paul would not have spent much time identifying different personality types. For him, Mark was a quitter. When the lad had set off with Paul and Barnabas, he seemed full of promise. However, it wasn't long before Mark returned home. Whatever the reason, it was lame as far as Paul was concerned.

So when Barnabas, Mark's cousin, wanted to give him a second chance, Paul was incensed. All the anger and hurt from Mark's 'desertion' was thrown into an argument so fierce that the two friends separated—and Mark disappears from the book of Acts.

However, Mark reappears in tantalizing remarks in the epistles, evidently active in mission and supporting God's people. Most movingly, the imprisoned Paul, late in life, asks Timothy: 'Mark can be very helpful to me, so please find him and bring him with you' (2 Timothy 4:11).

I am so glad that God is the God of the second, third and fourth chance! When I give up and mess up, when I run out of steam and fail to live up to my promises, that need not be the end. God can draw even these failures, even the disappointment of co-workers, even my sense of shame, into a beautiful story of grace. Because that is what he does: he uses broken people like me, if I will let him. I appreciate his goodness in a way I never could, had I not failed.

....

Is there something you have abandoned that God might like you to take up again?

For reasons to keep going when you are tempted to quit, read 1 Corinthians 15:57–58.

FB

Running out of steam

Seated in a window was a young man named Eutychus, who was sinking into a deep sleep as Paul talked on and on. When he was sound asleep, he fell to the ground from the third storey and was picked up dead.

How come some people have boundless energy and others feel tired just watching them? Are vigour and endless enthusiasm the marks of the super-spiritual?

Eutychus was a young lad but that night he did not have the 'oomph' to match Paul's pace. He was probably keen to be there. Paul was on a flying visit and had lots to say. Every moment was precious because he was leaving the next day.

The spirit was willing, but the flesh was weak! The meeting started in the evening. At midnight, Paul was still speaking. The many lamps made the room stuffy. Eutychus struggled to keep awake as Paul talked on. He sat by the window to get some fresh air, but eventually his tiredness got the better of him. Not only did he fall fast asleep, he also fell straight out of the window, landing with a thud—dead. He was not the last to drop off in a sermon, though the consequences were more serious for him than for most.

Did Luke see the funny side of what happened next? Paul interrupted his talk long enough to bring Eutychus back to life, but then went upstairs and continued until daybreak. A death and resurrection weren't going to stop him in his tracks! And yet, that was precisely the point: as they broke bread they were reminded of another death and resurrection. This was the God they loved and served—one who could bring life where there was death, a powerful God, whose care extended to the weary as well as the lively. He was always with them, although Paul was leaving. They were comforted and excited—with help from Eutychus!

....

If you are weary, what do you need to do to be energized once again?

For encouragement to rely on God's life-giving Spirit, read Romans 8:11.

FB

Investing for Jesus

I also remember the genuine faith of your mother Eunice. Your grandmother Lois had the same sort of faith, and I am sure that you have it as well... Since childhood, you have known the Holy Scriptures that are able to make you wise enough to have faith in Christ Jesus.

Changing nappies, preaching sermons, chairing board meetings, feeding the homeless, telling your daughter a bedtime story about Jesus. Is there a pecking order in these tasks? How would you rate them in terms of worth in a world of need?

I wonder how Eunice felt as she fed and clothed her baby. As she taught him to walk and talk, and sang salvation songs as lullabies, did she consider her role to be vital in spreading the gospel through Asia? As she told him the stories of Abraham, Sarah, David and Abigail, did she know she was moulding him into a man of God? As she kept the Jewish law, did she realize that she was modelling obedience to God? Eunice could never have imagined the contribution she made to the church simply by being a loving mother with a genuine faith.

We know just a little about Eunice. Life wasn't straightforward: her husband was Greek, and there may well have been frustrations in the household where not all shared her faith, first as a Jew and then as a Christian.

What is remarkable about Eunice is that, despite all the effort she invested in Timothy, she was prepared to let him go. Timothy was chosen to accompany Paul in planting churches because he was well-grounded in the scriptures and had a teachable heart. Saying goodbye to her son, knowing that persecution, prison and storms might await him, cannot have been easy. Paul's stoning in her town would have brought home vividly the fact that following Jesus was costly. Perhaps here is where her 'genuine faith' was tested the most.

....

How might your everyday activities be investments for God's kingdom?

To encourage you to make the most of what God has given you, read Matthew 25:14–30.

FB

Reviewing 'failure'

I think it is necessary to send back to you Epaphroditus, my brother, co-worker and fellow soldier, who is also your messenger, whom you sent to take care of my needs. For he longs for all of you and is distressed because you heard he was ill.

You plan an outreach event and nobody comes. You are part of a team to help the poor, but personality clashes break it up. You do a course you felt sure God wanted you to do, and fail the exams. You start a job, but can't complete it because you are unwell.

For Epaphroditus, it had all gone terribly wrong. He had been sent by the Philippians to help Paul, who was in prison. Paul still needed help but Epaphroditus was not to be the one to give it—all because he had fallen ill. Even worse was that, when he had physically recovered, he was beside himself with worry for the Philippians, who were so concerned about him. He'd become a liability rather than a help to Paul, who was sending him back so that everyone could be reassured.

Epaphroditus had not finished the task. Some Philippians might have wondered why he had been too weak to continue at Paul's side. 'Why was he not robust enough to hack it?' they might have asked.

So Paul insisted that Epaphroditus should be honoured, welcomed and loved. Giving little thought to his own comfort, he had risked his life. His practical help was like worship offered to God.

What moves me every time I think of Epaphroditus is this: as he returned to Philippi, physically well but emotionally vulnerable, he was probably carrying the letter we now read as Philippians. At his most wounded, he left us his most lasting legacy. He was the postman, used by God to deliver a letter that has comforted and challenged millions through two millennia.

Is there another way of looking at painful experiences that trouble you as 'failures'?

Read 2 Corinthians 1:3–9 to see how weaknesses might be reassessed.

FB

Walking in truth and love

The Lord's followers… speak openly of how you obey the truth…
You have always been faithful in helping other followers of the Lord…
They have told the church about your love.

Do you ever look round your church and imagine that God has given gifts to everyone apart from you? There are always people better at praying and cooking, smiling and organizing, and it is easy to feel that you have nothing to contribute. 'What can I do?' you ask yourself. 'I feel so inadequate and useless.'

That is why I am grateful for this mentor's memo, which is 3 John. Here we are allowed to get a glimpse into a very warm relationship between a church leader and a spiritual son. What is heart-warming is not that the writer is excited about Gaius' gifts but about his attitude. Very simply, Gaius walked in truth and in love: if love was one leg, truth was the other. His beliefs and his behaviour functioned as one and moved him forward as a Christian.

Because of this, Gaius had a vital part to play in the church's growth. He lived at a time when there were no complete Bibles, no commentaries or colleges. The good news of Jesus was spread by people travelling from place to place, preaching the gospel, setting up churches, mentoring leaders, writing letters and revisiting the believers.

Gaius loved the truth; he was caring; and so he was known throughout the area as someone who welcomed these missionaries, even the ones he did not know. He gave them hospitality, knowing that they would not be able to provide dinner in return. He encouraged them when they were tired and dispirited. He supplied what they needed so that they could be refreshed and invigorated to continue the work of mission throughout the area. So while Gaius did not travel and preach, his support made him an indispensable part of the mission team.

....

How do you support the work of mission? If God has not called
you to leave your own home, how might you encourage those who
do have that calling?

FB

Do you ever find God speaking to you through a verse that you can't get out of your mind? For me, as I write, that verse is 'God opposes the proud, but gives grace to the humble' (James 4:6, NIV). God is teaching me personally about pride and humility—but, after the focus of the last two weeks on some of God's unknown angels, it is encouraging to know that God gives his backing to humble people who might seem insignificant to the rest of the world.

Pride is a dangerous trap for people with power or a high profile—like the apostle Paul, who is the focus of our next fortnight's Bible readings. Paul was well qualified—a Jew of high standing and also a Roman citizen—but he didn't compare himself with others. He focused on Jesus:

Whatever was to my profit I now consider loss for the sake of Christ. What is more, I consider everything a loss compared to the surpassing greatness of knowing Christ Jesus my Lord, for whose sake I have lost all things. I consider them rubbish, that I may gain Christ and be found in him, not having a righteousness of my own that comes from the law, but that which is through faith in Christ—the righteousness that comes from God and is by faith (Philippians 3:7–9).

The devotional writer and Bible teacher Selwyn Hughes once said, 'You can never be really humble until you have a clear sense of identity. The true way to be humble is not to stoop until you are smaller than yourself, but to stand at your real height against some higher nature that will show you what the real smallness of your greatest greatness is.'

Self-awareness is vital. Paul's temporary blindness when Christ appeared to him on the road to Damascus must have brought his real stature and human weakness into sharp focus. Measured against Christ, Paul knew that his human achievements and abilities were meaningless.

Over the next two weeks, Rosemary Green will be helping us to consider Paul's prayer life, so that we can learn more about how this leading Christian prayed. What was his focus? What were his concerns? Let's learn from Paul and become women whose lives are steeped in prayer. The world might not notice us or might think we are insignificant—but there are centuries of evidence to show that praying women are powerful nation-changers.

A new relationship

He fell to the ground and heard a voice say to him, 'Saul, Saul, why do you persecute me?' 'Who are you, Lord?' Saul asked. 'I am Jesus, whom you are persecuting,' he replied. 'Now get up and go into the city, and you will be told what you must do.'

Sophie arrived in our church as a brand new Christian. During her gap year travels, she had seen a vision of Jesus in an Armenian cathedral. She knew little about Christianity but immediately responded to Jesus. Karim was a devoted Ugandan Muslim, a young imam. After leading the prayers in a mosque in Kampala, he twice heard a voice saying, 'I am Christ. I want you to follow me.' He chose to obey. Such stories match that of Paul's conversion from zealous persecutor to ardent Christian.

How do you tell the story of the journey that brought you to a living faith in Christ? Was it sudden or gradual? Was it in response to a sermon, to a friend's witness or to God's work within you? Often, many strands are intertwined. My own upbringing of intermittent churchgoing at home and frequent boarding school chapel services laid a 'faith fire' with paper and sticks but no spark. A growing yearning of 'Isn't there something more in Christianity?' made me ready to respond to a sermon that brought home the relevance of Jesus' death and resurrection, and showed me how to invite his Spirit into my life. The dormant fire was lit; my new life with Christ began. All our stories are different, and all are valid. Each one can speak of a growing relationship with Jesus.

The immediate effect seen by Paul's companions was his temporary blindness. The permanent effects were probably less obvious as he embarked on a life of prayer, obedience and evangelism. God told the reluctant Ananias, 'He is praying. In a vision he has seen...' (vv. 11–12). As a Pharisee, Paul was scrupulous in formal worship. Now he began to talk with the Jesus whom he had met. Communication in prayer is essential to developing our relationship with Christ.

....

Think of your early days as a Christian. Are you as eager now as you were then to talk with your new friend and to tell other people about him?

RG

35

Hearing God—for encouragement

One night God spoke to Paul in a vision. 'Do not be afraid; keep on speaking, do not be silent. For I am with you, and no one is going to attack and harm you, because I have many people in this city.'

Linda, not yet a Christian, was driving alone in her car, thinking about her troubles. A deep masculine voice spoke, sternly: 'My will, not yours.' Who was that? God? What did he mean? Over the years she realized how she was trying to control her life.

Years later, again in the car, she heard a younger, softer male voice: 'I am so sorry for what you are about to go through.' What was that about? That night her husband told her that he wanted a divorce. She could not cope with the loss of his love and companionship, so when a friend invited her to church her ears were open to hear about Jesus and his love for her. She knew it was true. Now, a year later, Linda is in my home group. It is exciting to watch her growth in her first year as a Christian.

When Paul arrived in Corinth, he already had considerable experience of opposition and assault in reaction to his preaching in many towns. The Lord's words of encouragement to him were very important: he could continue to preach and would see many converts in this multicultural, hedonistic city.

We do not all see visions or hear voices. God knows when these experiences of the living, personal God are particularly needed by an individual. But he speaks to us all through scripture. I am encouraged by the number of times we read, 'Don't be afraid.' It tells me that God understands how prone we are to fear but does not want us to be immobilized by it. We often read, 'Do not be afraid, for I am with you.' At other times his word is, in effect, 'Don't be afraid, for I have things under control.' He speaks through audible voices and through his written word.

Lord, thank you that you speak through scripture. May your words in the Bible be as alive and real to me as your words were to Paul and to Linda.

RG

Hearing God's voice—for mission

When God… was pleased to reveal his Son in me so that I might preach him among the Gentiles, my immediate response was not to consult any human being. I did not go up to Jerusalem to see those who were apostles before I was, but I went into Arabia. Later I returned to Damascus.

Paul was clear: the risen Jesus had commissioned him to preach the gospel to the Gentiles—a mission that he knew would stir up antagonism among his fellow Jews. So before he spent much time with his Christian family, he went away alone to spend time with his new Master. The theologians are less clear! They discuss at length just where he went, and why. I believe he needed to develop his relationship with Christ—and what substitute is there for spending time together when we want to grow a friendship? He needed, too, to know how he was to fulfil this mission.

When I am responsible for some sphere of Christian ministry, I usually spend much time in planning, even more in poring over details. Sadly, I spend less time in asking the Lord for his direction, either for the overall planning or for the details. My mind must be used, yes, but that mind must be consciously submitted to God. I know I am not very good at listening for his direction.

Paul was an activist but his activism was sustained and directed by his communication with God. I am glad to be writing these notes, because I know I have much to learn from Paul's prayer and the challenge it brings. Most of us do not see ourselves as active missionaries, but every one of us has a mission to fulfil as a witness to Jesus—to his truth, his character, and his desire to be in every life. It is helpful to start every day with a prayer like this: 'Lord, please help me stay in touch with you today. May I be alert to any opportunity you give me to demonstrate you or to speak about you.'

....

Lord, I really do want to please you in my life. Please show me how to pray, how to listen, how to live, how to speak.

Read Acts 13:1–4; 16:6–10 to see two occasions when God gave clear directions.

RG

In times of stress

After they had been severely flogged, they were thrown into prison, and the jailer was commanded to guard them carefully... He put them in the inner cell and fastened their feet in the stocks. About midnight Paul and Silas were praying and singing hymns to God, and the other prisoners were listening to them.

Unjustly accused, punished without fair trial, whipped, imprisoned and locked in stocks. Many of us would call out in desperate prayer, 'Lord, this isn't fair!' Not so Paul and Silas. Praise and prayer were their response (and not just to impress the other prisoners—though impressed they were). Then God acted in a mighty way, with an earthquake that unlocked the prison doors and led to the warder's conversion.

Six years ago, four men with machine guns burst into the grounds of a school for missionaries' children in Pakistan. The children (three of my grandchildren among them) and teachers huddled under desks for two hours. One boy wrote afterwards, 'What encouraged me throughout the attack was that people were praying, singing to God all around me. Tim passed round a book that said "Prisoners of war, God is with you."' A girl in another classroom wrote of the person who read Psalm 46 aloud: 'God is our refuge and strength, an ever-present help in trouble.' Then others started singing choruses, including 'This is the day that the Lord has made'. She continued, 'I almost laughed. It sounded so totally out of place, so happy and simple in all the terrifying evil. But, as I thought about it, it was the Lord's day. He made it, and it was his.'

We rarely experience trauma as intense as did Paul and Silas or those children in Pakistan. When things go wrong, we easily get discouraged, we often complain, and we might pray. Next time I am under stress, I would like instead to turn to God's encouragements in the Bible, to sing, to praise a God who is always good and faithful, to entrust my problems to a God who is, despite appearances, in control.

....

Lord, when things seem bad, please help me to remember that you are the faithful God whom I can praise for your goodness in my situation—even when I am not ready to thank you for it.

RG

Thanksgiving

Do not be anxious about anything, but in every situation, by prayer and petition, with thanksgiving, present your requests to God. And the peace of God, which transcends all understanding, will guard your hearts and your minds in Christ Jesus.

Mummy: 'Jemima, Auntie Joan's got a present for you. What do you say?' Jemima: 'Thank you, Auntie.' We work hard at teaching our children to say 'thank you', but we often forget the same lesson ourselves. A gift, an act of kindness, a job well done—each one deserves a simple word of thanks.

Last Sunday, I visited an elderly woman in a care home. She is very forgetful, sometimes cantankerous, even physically aggressive. Afterwards I was talking with the carers who were on duty that afternoon, appreciating their stressful work (which I know I couldn't do). One of them commented, 'Visitors rarely thank us.' I think that is sad. Complaints, yes; being taken for granted, yes; but not thanks.

These verses are not only a help in stress but a stimulus to thankfulness. Thanksgiving can be woven into every conversation, in our human relationships and with God. Paul did this himself. Glance through the beginning of his letters and see how often he thanks God for the recipients—even the ones he is going to rebuke. Philippians 1:3 is just one example: 'I thank my God every time I remember you.' His thanks came before his requests to God or his reprimands to his disciples.

I am usually ready to thank God when I notice a specific answer to prayer, but there are many things in life that I take for granted. I regularly say grace at meals, but it easily becomes a formality rather than heartfelt gratitude, forgetting millions in the world who are starving. I may pray for victims of earthquakes but forget to thank God for my comfortable, secure home. I may complain at a grandson's behaviour but fail to thank God for my many grandchildren. May we be thankful people.

....

Have you ever sung this chorus? It is old but not outdated. 'Count your blessings, name them one by one. Count your blessings, see what God has done. Count your blessings, name them one by one, and it will surprise you what the Lord has done' (J. Oatman Jr).

RG

Praying for other Christians

This is my prayer: that your love may abound more and more in knowledge and depth of insight, so that you may be able to discern what is best and may be pure and blameless for the day of Christ, filled with the fruit of righteousness that comes through Jesus Christ.

On Wednesday we saw Paul in prison in Philippi. After his release he moved on south, leaving Luke in charge of the infant church. He probably visited the Philippians again twice, some years later. By the time Paul wrote this letter to them, he was again in prison, this time in Rome. He shows far more concern for the converts than he does for himself, though, expressing gratitude for the many gifts they have sent him (1:4–5; 4:15–18).

What is our focus when we pray for other Christians? I think of a bi-weekly meeting in our church, set up to pray for individuals who are ill or in other difficult situations. It is a very caring group of people, who regularly give practical service with meals and by driving people to hospital. We pray for the physical needs, for the medical care, for healing, for resolution of stressful situations. But rarely do we pray about the spiritual implications, that the illnesses and other pressures may lead people into deeper dependence on Christ or further refine their characters.

How did Paul pray for these Christians? Read again the verses at the top of this page. He prays that they may grow in love; he prays that increasing understanding and insight may lead to holiness of character. Physical needs do matter, but our relationship with Christ and the development of character are even more important to God. Paul's prayer is one that we can use to pray for any Christians—or we can turn it into the first person to pray for ourselves: 'I pray that my love may abound more and more…'.

....

Use Paul's prayer now to pray for people you know. Pray that they 'may be able to discern what is best' as they make decisions, and that they 'may be filled with the fruit of righteousness' to endure pain with patience.

RG

A farewell prayer

When Paul had finished speaking, he knelt down with all of them and prayed. They all wept as they embraced him and kissed him. What grieved them most was his statement that they would never see his face again. Then they accompanied him to the ship.

Paul was en route to Jerusalem, in a hurry to arrive by Pentecost. To save time, he sent a message for the church leaders from nearby Ephesus to come to the port of Miletus. After reminding them of the integrity of his own ministry (vv. 17–27), he warned them and encouraged them for their responsibilities. I guess that their distress over the thought that they would never see him again either hindered their ability to listen or sharpened their eagerness to absorb his last words. They were losing not only their itinerant 'bishop' but also a friend they loved.

Then they knelt and prayed, right where they were, by the harbour, unashamed by having spectators. Their readiness to pray with a friend, anywhere, is a habit worth cultivating. It is easy to say after a conversation, 'I'll remember you… I'll think of you… I'll pray for you' and it is even easier to forget afterwards. On the phone, on the pavement, in a friend's living room, at the pick-your-own fruit farm: all are places where I have prayed, aloud, with another person. I remember a dozen people in a tight huddle in Durban airport when we were about to leave and other friends had just flown in. Years later, I bumped into an acquaintance by the toilets in another airport; we prayed then and there for her impending interview. I find that if I have prayed with a person on the spot, I am more likely to remember to pray later.

How did they pray? The chapter provides some clues: they prayed about their gratitude for Paul's ministry, their grief at his departure, the uncertainty of his future, his concern for the expected attacks on the church and his own determination to work hard, to serve others and to trust God.

....

Think of the past 24 hours—the people you have been with, and images you have seen on the TV. Each one can be a cause for thanksgiving or intercession.

RG

Armed for a fight

Take the helmet of salvation and the sword of the Spirit, which is the word of God. And pray in the Spirit on all occasions with all kinds of prayers and requests. With this in mind, be alert and always keep on praying for all the Lord's people.

Last week I bought a birthday present for my six-year-old grandson—a set of plastic Roman soldier's armour, with helmet, breastplate, shield and sword. He will certainly playfight with his brothers; I hope his parents will also use it to show him these verses.

Our battles are far from playfighting. Yesterday's reading in Acts 20 included Paul's warning about attacks on godly beliefs, and today I have read of a physical assault on a Nigerian bishop. Behind these attacks are the dark forces of evil. Paul wants us to be alert to these forces, whether subtle or overt, and to be armed with the qualities to resist them.

The 'full armour of God' includes truth and integrity, then righteousness—both the righteousness that comes from being forgiven by God and our aim to grow in holiness. Next comes the willingness to step out to communicate the gospel, followed by faith—trusting the God who is supreme. When I first met a woman who was dominated by evil spirits, I recognized the power of evil as never before. I learnt more that day about the power of Christ than I had through any other experience. The last two pieces of armour are salvation—our certainty in God's power to save—and God's word. If we are rooted in scripture, we can use it as a weapon, as Jesus did when he faced the devil in the desert.

Last but not least, we are to pray 'in the Spirit'. Some people equate this with praying in tongues, but that is only one dimension. A wider definition is 'prayer enabled by God's Spirit', prayer directed by his bird's-eye view. We are to pray about anything and everything—at any time, in any place—and for everyone, especially other Christians, as we stay alert to 'the powers of this dark world' (v. 12).

....

Ask God to show you if your armour is defective and how you can better keep in touch with the commander.

Read Romans 8:26–27 to go deeper in prayer in the Spirit.

RG

'Pray for me'

Pray also for me, that whenever I speak, words may be given me so that I will fearlessly make known the mystery of the gospel.

When you ask someone to pray for you, what sort of requests do you make? Paul did not often ask for prayer for himself. When he did, it was not for himself personally but that he might be effective and fearless in evangelism. And remember: this letter to the Ephesians was written not when he was free to travel and preach in synagogue and marketplace, but when he was in prison.

It is the same with Colossians, also written from prison in Rome. In Colossians 4:3–4, Paul prays that God will 'open a door' for the gospel message, and his prayer was answered. Onesimus the runaway slave, for one, 'became my son while I was in chains' (Philemon 10). There were probably many others who became Christians through Paul in prison. Certainly, in Philippi, 'the whole palace guard' knew that his imprisonment was because of his faith in Christ (Philippians 1:13).

I find two challenges for myself. First, there is Paul's example. I can make Paul's words my own and ask others to pray that I may have greater boldness in speaking to non-believers about Jesus, whatever my situation. Second, I can commit myself to pray for missionaries, overseas or in this country.

I can pray, too, for Christians persecuted for their faith in their own countries. I read this today in the magazine of Christian Solidarity Worldwide: 'On 18 April one German and two Turkish Christians were killed in a Christian publishing house in south-east Turkey. Two were found tied to chairs by their hands and legs with their throats cut. The second Turkish citizen died later in hospital from multiple stab wounds. Initial reports attribute the murders to right-wing nationalists who had previously threatened... the bookshop.' Such is the persecution that faces our fellow Christians in many parts of the world.

....

Lord, please forgive me that my witness is so feeble, despite the comfort and safety of my situation. Please help me to take risks in speaking about my faith, and to remember to pray for Christians facing intense persecution.

RG

Praying for the Middle East

Brothers and sisters, my heart's desire and prayer to God for the Israelites is that they may be saved… I urge, then, first of all, that petitions, prayers, intercession and thanksgiving be made for everyone—for kings and all those in authority, that we may lead peaceful and quiet lives in all godliness and holiness.

Iraq, Iran, Lebanon, Israel, Palestine—one or another is regularly headline news, and the news is never of peace. Even during the tumultuous acclaim in Iraq for the success of the national football team in the 2007 Asian Cup, there were attacks and deaths.

I started thinking about today's reading with regard to Paul's concern for his fellow Jews. Although his prime calling was to take the gospel to the Gentiles, when he arrived in a new place he almost invariably went first to speak in the synagogue. I believe that if he were to look at Israel 20 centuries later, with more emphasis on its life as a secular nation than as the people of God, he would pray for them in the same way: 'My heart's desire and prayer to God… is that they may be saved.' We can pray for the nation of Israel in the same way.

Then my thoughts turned to the whole geographical area, with its unending tensions. We hear the news through the media. We pray for fighting to cease, for political resolution, for the safety of those who live, work and fight in those countries. But how often do we pray for the hearts and minds of men, women and children to be won for Christ, who alone can bring reconciliation? Do we pray for those in authority to lead the Middle East in a way that may enable the gospel to spread more easily? Do we pray for the Christians in these lands?

In recent years, a large proportion of Palestine's Christian population has emigrated to find a safer, more peaceful environment in which to live. It is for their benefit but results in the impoverishment of a country that is special to Jew, Muslim and Christian alike.

....

I ask God to give me—and you—new insight and new passion to pray for all people in the Middle East; above all, that they may come to follow Jesus.

RG

An outpouring of praise

Praise be to the God and Father of our Lord Jesus Christ, who has blessed us in the heavenly realms with every spiritual blessing in Christ.

The first three chapters of this letter are a wonderful intermingling of praise, intercession and doctrine. As we look at Paul's outpouring in prayer in these chapters, we will see the strands woven together.

What is the most memorable waterfall you have ever seen? The Victoria Falls in Zambia or the Niagara Falls in Canada? High Force in Teesdale or Aira Force in the Lake District? The water cascades with endless power in fascinating patterns. Paul's praise is like that as his wonder at the richness of God's blessing tumbles out—all in one long sentence in the original Greek. He is full of joy at God's lavish generosity. So what does he see as the cause for such praise?

God chose us (vv. 4, 11) long before we ever chose to follow him. He chose us 'before the creation of the world': isn't that amazing? He chose us to live holy lives: what a standard!

He adopted us as his children (v. 5). It is as if God picked us up as street kids and made us part of his royal family.

He redeems us (v. 7). The image here is of a pawnbroker. The rightful owner, God the Father, has bought us back at the immense cost of Jesus' death, 'through his blood'.

He enlightened us (v. 9) and has shown us his eternal purposes.

He included us 'in Christ' (v. 13), with all the privileges of that relationship.

He sealed us with the Holy Spirit (v. 13). A seal was a mark of ownership, of personal identification, so we belong to him. The Spirit is also a deposit guaranteeing more to come, like the down-payment we may make on the purchase of a car—a promise of full payment in the future.

....

Think how impoverished we would be if God had not chosen us— if he had left us in the gutter, abandoned us in the shop, left us in the dark, with no understanding and no Holy Spirit to give us life within. Then join in Paul's praise and use it as your own prayer.

RG

Enjoying our inheritance—now

I pray that the eyes of your heart may be enlightened in order that you may know the hope to which he has called you, the riches of his glorious inheritance in his people, and his incomparably great power for us who believe.

What are the first things you ask when you pray for your parents, siblings, husband, offspring, neighbours, colleagues or church? Many of my prayers are practical, earthbound. They are for good health, wise parenting, solutions to financial problems, guidance, and so on. They are small and petty concerns, compared with Paul's vision as he prayed for Christians. His focus in yesterday's reading was praise to God for all the ways in which he has already blessed us, finishing with the Holy Spirit who is the foretaste of what is to come. That is the 'reason' (v. 15) that moves him on to pray that we might not miss out on the fullness of the eternal riches that we can begin to experience *now*.

Paul prays that we may know God better, which was his own passion for himself, as we will see on Saturday. He prays that we may be sure of all the riches we share with all Christian believers, past, present and future. He prays that we may experience 'his incomparably great power' in our lives. Verses 19 and 20 are among my 'Wow!' verses in the Bible. The power that raised Jesus from the dead and lifted him to his rightful place in heaven—that is the power on which we can draw, in which we can live, here and now. That is amazing! I don't pretend that I remember it every minute of my day, but I wish I did.

This puts my small prayers into new perspective. If we really know, experience and live out all that God has for us, we will not become 'so heavenly minded that we are no earthly use'. Rather, the jigsaw pieces of life on earth will fit more easily into the big picture of God's heavenly purposes and riches.

....

Use verses 17 to 20 to pray both for yourself and for other people, either in Paul's words or your own: 'I ask you, glorious Father, to give me the Spirit of wisdom and revelation'; 'I pray for Susan, and ask that she may come to know you better.'

RG

Knowing God's love

For this reason I kneel before the Father, from whom his whole family in heaven and on earth derives its name… I pray that you, being rooted and established in love, may have power, together with all the saints, to grasp how wide and long and high and deep is the love of Christ.

Our four offspring and 14 grandchildren are widely dispersed, and it is rare for our whole family to get together, but our recent golden wedding celebration brought 19 out of 24 under one roof for a weekend. We watched with joy the relationships between different generations and different families. It gave me a new glimpse of the Father's 'whole family in heaven and on earth' to which we belong. Paul makes two big requests for the members of this family. First, he asks for the Spirit of Christ, resident in us, to strengthen us with power. Then he prays for us to have a sure knowledge and deep experience of God's immense love.

Over 20 years ago, I realized how little I knew about loving other people. I read repeatedly 1 Corinthians 13. With one hand metaphorically open, I prayed for God (through gritted teeth) to give me that love. My other fist remained tightly clenched: 'Not really. I'd have to change and to give.' Eventually God broke through. At home in England while my husband lay in hospital in South Africa with meningitis, my shyness and pride initially resisted my friends' pleas to love me and help me. At last I recognized my frailty, and my defences collapsed. God's love flowed from my friends to me and was then planted in me, sprouting a fresh love for Christ—and loving other people became natural, not hard. That was one of the most transforming experiences of my life.

Finally, think about verses 20 and 21. God can do what we ask… more than we ask… immeasurably more than we ask… more than we ask or even imagine. How? Through his power *at work in us*. He works through us to enable our prayers to be answered.

....

Many Christians can say in their heads 'God loves me', but without assurance in their hearts. Pray verses 18 and 19 for yourself and for others.

RG

Knowing Christ

I want to know Christ and the power of his resurrection and the fellowship of sharing in his sufferings, becoming like him in his death, and so, somehow, to attain to the resurrection from the dead.

I have the privilege of being involved in much Christian ministry. What thrills me most is to see God at work, changing someone's life, and to know that I have been a very junior partner with the Lord in his work. But I find it easy for my love of ministry for Jesus to override my love of Jesus himself. We may enjoy knowing that we are not merely 'Sunday Christians' but Monday-to-Saturday Christians as well, but it is a small step to the pride of the Pharisee who, in Jesus' story, prayed, 'God, I thank you that I am not like other men… I fast twice a week' (Luke 18:11–12). That sort of pride quenches love for God.

Paul was not like that. He had a passion for evangelism, that others might come to follow Jesus, but he had an even deeper passion to know Christ himself, more and more—'the surpassing greatness of knowing Christ' (v. 8). He didn't mind what that passion cost him. It had already cost him his reliance on his impeccable Jewish pedigree and his Pharisaic zeal for ritualistic righteousness (vv. 4–6). It had taken him into danger and persecution. He was currently in a Roman jail. He didn't know what lay ahead of him on earth, but of one thing he was sure: he longed to know Christ better on earth and to be with him in heaven. That was what fuelled the vitality of all his prayer. That was what was behind the secret of his 'being content in any and every situation' (4:12). That was the mainstay of his ever-growing relationship with the Lord.

If you feel able, pray with Paul verses 8–9 from our reading today (based on the Good News Bible):

....

'I reckon everything as complete loss for the sake of what is so much more valuable—knowing you, Christ Jesus my Lord. For your sake I am willing to throw everything away and consider it all garbage, so that I may gain you and be completely united with you.'

RG

If you can, extend your prayer time today in light of what you've read over the past two weeks.

Think back to the 'armour of God' in Ephesians 6 (see notes for 5 October). It's interesting to realize that all four of the items of 'clothing' in the armour can be summed up in one person—Jesus.

- Jesus himself said, 'I am... the truth' (John 14:6).
- Jeremiah prophesied the coming of Jesus as 'The Lord Our Righteousness' (Jeremiah 23:6).
- Zechariah prayed of the baby Jesus, 'My eyes have seen your salvation' (Luke 2:30).
- Paul says of Jesus, 'He himself is our peace'—the one who enables us to preach reconciliation (Ephesians 2:14).

This means that if we, like Paul, devote ourselves to knowing Christ, we will find ourselves ever more securely clothed in God's armour. Then we will grow in confidence as we use the shield of faith and the sword of God's word.

Open your heart to Jesus now: speak to him of your joys and concerns and listen to hear him give you his guidance, encouragement or loving correction.

As you bring your thinking more in line with his, ask him to strengthen you in his truth... righteousness... salvation... readiness to proclaim peace. Thank him for the gift of your faith, however small you think it may be. Lift it up as a shield over your life. Thank him for your knowledge of his word: remember that your sword is being sharpened as you read part of the Bible each day and get to know Jesus better— the living Word!

As we have seen, Paul knew the power of words. His prayers announced a new reality for people. For example, when he prayed that the Ephesians would 'grasp how wide and long and high and deep is the love of Christ', Paul expected their lives to be transformed. Knowing God's love was top priority for Paul, but notice what he said in 1 Corinthians 14:1: 'Follow the way of love *and* eagerly desire spiritual gifts, *especially* the gift of prophecy' (TNIV).

In the next series of notes, Alie Stibbe will be highlighting this gift of prophecy. Caricatures paint pictures of prophets as bearded and strange—although, if Paul's challenge is taken seriously, we will all be gifted prophetically.

The type of prophets Alie encourages us to be are people like St Francis of Assisi, who is quoted as saying 'Preach the gospel at all times. Where necessary, use words.' As legend has it, Francis used actions rather than mere words to show that he was renouncing his family's wealth to follow Christ, even leaving behind the clothes provided by his father, a rich cloth merchant. Francis founded the Franciscan Order, based on a simple statment by Jesus: 'Leave all and follow me'. He continued living in poverty throughout his life, visiting hospitals, serving the poor and the sick, showing the richness of life free from materialism.

Contemporary prophets are also people who challenge the status quo, whose words or actions usher in change. Are you living prophetically? Do your actions show others that there is a different, better way to live? Christians can be known as people with a list of 'don't's. Instead, let's be known for the positive, prophetic difference that we make—like our forebears who helped found the welfare state, and started hospitals, schools, hospices and a host of other organizations dedicated to loving, caring and social change. We might not be Florence Nightingale, William Wilberforce or Lord Shaftesbury, but our actions and attitudes at work, out shopping, talking over the garden fence with a neighbour, even driving, can all speak volumes and move mountains.

Looking for alternatives?

So if anyone is in Christ, there is a new creation: everything old has passed away; see, everything has become new!

This year, many churches in the UK are joining the Hope 2008 initiative, which aims to focus on various aspects of Christian hope throughout the year, emphasizing community action and social justice. In the next two weeks, I want to share with you some insights into the prophetic nature of such an initiative, in terms of both the actions and the words that will inevitably spring from it.

When I was invited to write these notes, I was just finishing writing my thesis on the function of 'prophetic imagination' in the religious writings of one of Norway's greatest lay preachers, Hans Nielsen Hauge (1771–1824). Much of what I want to say springs from the insights into prophecy that I gained while I was doing that research—but I promise to keep things simple.

The main thing I want to highlight is what Walter Brueggemann described as 'the task of [a] prophetic ministry [such as Hope 2008]… to nurture, nourish, and evoke a consciousness and perception alternative to the consciousness and perception of the dominant culture around us' (*The Prophetic Imagination*, Fortress Press, 2001). This is just a fancy way of saying that as Christians we are called to 'go against the flow', to demonstrate a different way of doing things. As a result, people who are unthinkingly living their lives according to the unspoken rules of contemporary secular culture are put into a position where they can begin to question the way they live and what they believe. This may give people a window of opportunity to see or imagine what life might be like if they thought and acted differently. Facing up to such a life choice is a momentous challenge for anybody—it can be scary to put off the old and put on the new.

....

Lord, fire my imagination by your Holy Spirit. Open my eyes to see what stops me becoming all that you want me to be.

Read 2 Peter 3:13. How real is this promise in your imagination?

AS

Endings and beginnings

This one thing I do: forgetting what lies behind and straining forward to what lies ahead, I press on towards the goal.

When our friend Katherine stopped in the middle of the street in a Ugandan village to gather up a man thrown out of his home to die in indescribable indignity, she performed a prophetic act that called for an end to the way the ill and dying are treated in that society. Such an act criticizes the status quo and silently shouts that 'enough is enough'. Katherine took the man home, bathed him and tended him for the remaining twelve hours of his life without concern for her own health. Her act of compassion and sacrifice is one that calls for a new beginning, in that it demonstrates an alternative way of caring for the terminally ill even in the most primitive of surroundings. Katherine's act was prophetic imagination in action. It called for both an ending and a beginning. It 'criticized'—calling into question the status quo—and 'energized', showing a new way of doing things.

The words spoken and actions taken by Christians in the community projects of Hope 2008 can help people to see life differently. It is important for us to understand that such 'prophetic imagination' demands two things: an ending and a beginning. In order to bring a new way of thinking and acting into being, an old way of thinking and acting has to end.

In our own lives, too, we need to understand that there are no new beginnings without something ending. If God is calling you to new horizons, you can be sure that he is calling you to turn your back on old horizons. Learning to recognize what has to end and having the courage to let go is always a challenge, but it is one that we all have to face if we want to live radical lives in Christ.

....

Lord, I want to keep the familiarity of the old while I embrace the uncertainty of the new. Help me to forget what lies behind and press forward in you.

AS

Where there's hope, there's life

He has delivered us … and he will deliver us again. On him we have set our hope that he will continue to deliver us.

Yesterday I suggested that 'prophetic imagination' (the kind of speech and action that calls into being an alternative way of thinking and acting) involves two facets: endings and beginnings. Prophetic speech and action that calls for endings acts to *criticize* the way things are in contemporary society—and there is no other way to describe it, despite the fact that we are under such pressure to be tolerant of others' differences.

It is an unavoidable fact that God has never been tolerant of certain attitudes and behaviour: his standards of holiness and justice are the same yesterday, today and for ever. God, by nature, will always stand against political, economic and religious oppression, and prophetic speech and prophetic action will by nature criticize such oppression with the intention of disempowering it. This sort of prophetic speech was used by the Old Testament prophets when they spoke out against the people of Israel after they had turned their backs on God. Some of the prophets also undertook prophetic actions—like walking around naked for three years to symbolize Israel's shame (not an action that I would recommend today!)

On the other hand, prophetic speech and action that calls for new beginnings acts to *empower* new ways of being and doing, to bring them into existence. The prophetic speech and action that springs from the empowering aspect of prophetic imagination is characterized by hope. Hope is full of spiritual potential energy to change things for the better; it is also a subversive quality in that it enables us to refuse the notion that present circumstances are unchangeable. When we understand this dynamic quality of hope, we see why hope is essential for human existence and why, without it, we perish.

....

Lord, you are the hope of the hopeless. Help me to find my hope in you, even when circumstances may seem at their darkest.

AS

Actions speak louder than words

'Not by might nor by power, but by my Spirit, says the Lord Almighty.

People usually associate prophecy with the speaking of words. The interesting thing is that effective prophecy can be an action just as much as, if not more than, it can be words. The common denominator between truly prophetic action and truly prophetic speech in the Christian sense is that both are inspired and empowered by God's Holy Spirit. Although we often find the word 'prophetic' used by secular commentators to describe secular social action, this is not how we should understand a truly Holy Spirit-inspired, prophetic act. It is so much more than the kind of charitable initiative that a good-hearted person or group of people might get into their minds to undertake.

It might help to remember the words of the Lord through the prophet Zechariah to Zerubbabel when he was called to rebuild the temple: 'Not by might nor by power, but by my Spirit' (v. 6). Rebuilding the temple was a prophetic act, not only because the building itself had great symbolic significance for the people of Israel, but because the act of rebuilding would be empowered by God's Spirit and it would engender hope.

If you are involved in a Hope 2008 community initiative this year, don't forget to welcome the presence and power of the Holy Spirit into your project. It doesn't matter if that project is washing graffiti off car park walls or picking up litter—if it is done in the power of the Spirit, it is much more effective than the same act done in our own strength, because the Spirit-empowered act changes things in the spiritual realm in a way that we can't begin to understand.

....

Lord, may the acts of loving sacrifice that I make be indwelt by the power of your Spirit, or I know they are in vain.

Read 1 Samuel 15:22. What kind of sacrifice might obeying the voice of the Lord mean for you?

AS

Speaking out of action

Dear children, let us not love with words or tongue but with actions and in truth.

It is quite easy to see how an action can be prophetic, because, when the task or project is completed, we can stand back and admire how tidy the elderly woman's garden is or how bright the playground apparatus looks now that it has been painted. We can see the immediate results. We can also see the secondary results in the eyes of the people whose lives have been affected: the elderly woman might be in tears or bring out a tray of tea and biscuits; the children and (despite the occasional cynic) the parents who use the playground will probably be thrilled that the area is now clean, safe and a cheerful place in which to play. Actions like these lead to the inevitable question, 'Why did you do that for me?' How do you answer a question like that without sounding trite or getting overly theological?

I think the simple answer is that the Father calls us, through Jesus, to love one another as he has loved us. That means laying down our lives for others by making sacrificial acts—which are inherently prophetic—whether that means giving up your bank holiday weekend or committing time and energy on a more consistent and regular basis. In my opinion, the latter demonstrates the real truth of love in action because it doesn't 'hit and run', it stays and suffers with the person or people who are the focus of our love in Christ.

Are you willing for your one-off action to lead you to go back and maintain that elderly woman's garden or to invite her to share your Christmas meal? In that respect, Hope 2008 is as much about changing and challenging us as individuals and churches as it is about challenging and changing our local community.

....

Lord, arouse your compassion in my heart and change me, so that I can learn to commit to others for the sake of your love.

AS

Words can do things

See, the former things have taken place, and new things I declare; before they spring into being I announce them to you.

Yesterday we focused on how actions can be prophetic: they demonstrate the way in which situations can be different, and the commitment to ongoing acts of mercy challenges us to change and become different people. Also, words can be a form of action. Words can change things even when no physical action takes place.

Think about: 'I now declare you man and wife. What God has joined together let no one separate.' With those words, a man and a woman cease to be two individuals and become 'one': a marriage has taken place. On the outside, nothing seems to have changed—there are still two people standing there—but something has changed in the spiritual realm, something that we can not see, and a new reality has come into being. The interesting thing is that not just anybody can say those words and perform a marriage.

While on holiday in Greece, one of our sons found a young couple getting 'cosy' in the hotel cloakrooms. In his own inimitable way he announced, 'You two need to get married! I'm the son of a vicar, so I pronounce you man and wife!' Later we all laughed. Why? Because everyone knows that that kind of statement from someone like our son is null and void, as he doesn't have the authority to change anything by saying those words.

Look at today's verse. The ultimate authority is God: when he declares 'new things', he has the authority and the power to bring them into being. When God declares a new thing, usually through prophecy, we can have confidence that something has changed in the spiritual realm and a new season is about to begin, even if we can't see it.

Lord, give me deeper understanding of how your words can speak new realities into being.

Read Genesis 27:1–40 to see the negative consequences of words spoken by a person with authority.

AS

Words achieve their purpose

So is my word that goes out from my mouth: it will not return to me empty, but will accomplish what I desire and achieve the purpose for which I sent it.

Words can do things; words can change situations. Unfortunately, words can change things for the worse as well as for the better. The classic situation is described in Proverbs 14:1: 'The wise woman builds her house, but with her own hands the foolish one tears hers down.' Knowing what I know about myself and other women, the tearing down and building up is not done with physical actions but with words. The most brief, uncalled-for comment can wound a child for life.

I still remember something my father said to me when I was very young, that I am convinced is the root of my insecurities and the striving I have put myself through over the years. He didn't mean to say what he said—the words fell off his tongue in a moment of pressure—but words have power to achieve their intrinsic intention, even if the human speaker spoke them unthinkingly and probably didn't mean them.

Prophetic words also contain an element of criticism, because, as we read a few days ago, something new cannot usually come into being unless something old is torn down. But we need to be careful with criticism. It is much better to focus on words that build up, because in achieving their purpose they also have a subtle, hidden power to replace the old thing quietly with something new. I believe this is why we find an emphasis on 'encouraging words' in the descriptions of prophecy that we find in the New Testament (for example, 1 Corinthians 14:31). So when we are at home, or out on a Hope 2008 social action project, we can speak out positive words so that the new thing God wants to bring into being is hastened.

....

Lord, help me to understand the hidden intentions in the idle words that thoughtlessly slip from my lips.

Read Proverbs 11:11 to see the effect of speaking positive words over your community

AS

Speak out for a change

You will also decree a thing, and it will be established for you; and light will shine on your ways.

There is no way I can write about the power of words to change situations and bring into being new realities without taking a look at today's verse. I have always lived with some suspicion of Christians who take Jesus' words in Matthew 18:19 to the extreme, as I have met many people who treat God like a vending machine. However, the more I have come to understand about the power of words, especially when words are used by people with the right authority, the more I have had to concede that what we say on earth can change things in the heavenly realms and subsequently in our own earthly experience.

Yesterday's extra reading verse was Proverbs 11:11, which, in case you didn't read it, says, 'Through the blessing of the upright a city is exalted' (TNIV). As opposed to asking God for a new Mercedes-Benz, I have no problem believing that if, as 'upright believers', we get together and speak a blessing over our city—decree over it that God's blessing will be poured out on its people and its environment—something will change in the spiritual realm that will cause change in the physical realm. If we are 'the upright' (which means right with God and walking in his ways), then we do have the spiritual authority to decree things, to speak them out and expect something to change.

When you are out on a social action project, or maybe just walking to the shops, decree God's blessing on the people you see and the places you pass through. Speaking out causes change. Don't worry about strange looks—you could be talking into a 'hands-free' mobile phone for all anyone knows!

....

Lord, help me to appreciate the spiritual authority you have given your children, and show me how I can use it to speak your kingdom into being.

Read Colossians 2:9–10 to gain some understanding of the authority we have in Christ.

AS

God-breathed words

'The Spirit of the Lord will come on you in power, and you will prophesy with them; and you will be changed into a different person.'

Prophetic words can change things not just because words have an
inherent purpose of their own, or that the person speaking them has
been given spiritual authority by the Lord, but mainly because the
speaker is indwelt and the spoken words are inspired by God's Holy
Spirit. He is the main agent for change in prophetic ministry: in fact,
he is the main agent for change in all Christian ministry, which, if it
is authentic, is by nature prophetic.

It is the indwelling of the Spirit that makes the difference when we
agree on a course of action in Jesus' name. The believer who is
indwelt and led by the Spirit finds it impossible to treat God like a
divine vending machine; the heart of a true prophet grieves with a
reflection of the depth of grief that is found only in the heart of God.
The grieving prophetic heart thus finds it impossible to decree blessing purely for its own sake, but is consumed by proclaiming the
Lord's salvation to all who will hear, with an intensity of compassion
that few of us ever experience.

This is what is meant by today's verse, when we read that when
the Lord's Spirit comes on you in power and you prophesy, then 'you
will be changed into a different person'. I am not sure that we have
to develop grieving hearts before we can prophesy; I think the Spirit,
the grieving and the words that change reality come as an intricately
entwined entity as opposed to a stepwise package. It is a bold
believer who asks the Lord to break their heart with grief for others
so that they can minister prophetically. May we all be that bold!

....

*Lord, like Hosea, by your Spirit I want to know that 'my heart is
changed within me; all my compassion is aroused' for those to
whom you would extend your mercy.*

AS

How does prophecy change things?

'This is what the Lord says to you: "Do not be afraid or discouraged because of this vast army. For the battle is not yours, but God's."'

After looking at the power of Spirit-indwelt words to change things, we need to see a real example. There are all types of prophecy in the Bible, but those that act to change things for the better belong to a big group called 'announcements of salvation'. These kinds of words instil hope, energize, empower and encourage the listener to realize that God has more for us than our perception of present reality.

Many prophetic sayings have two parts: they predict something or admonish people to do something, and they give a reason why. In today's reading (vv. 15–17), the Lord uses Jeremiah to tell King Jehoshaphat and all who live in Judah and Jerusalem not to be afraid or discouraged because of the vast army that is facing them. And why? 'For the battle is not yours, but God's.' How does this change things?

First, it faces up to the apparent reality of the situation, acknowledging that the people are afraid and that the enemy army is large. Then, it exhorts them not to give in to their fear. This raises their expectations on a human level, just through the power of the way words of exhortation act in the mind. Finally, the prophet gives the spiritual reason: 'For the battle is not yours, but God's.' This changes everything for the listener who believes and trusts in a big God— because the bigger the enemy army, the bigger will be God's victory. The words not only change perception, but also raise spiritual awareness and faith. Now we are willing to let the Lord do what he wants through us, because we know he is on our side and, from what we know of his character, we can expect a promised victory.

Lord, I often see the glass half empty, not half full. Let your words change the way I see things and raise my faith in you.

Read 1 Samuel 1:17. How do you think Eli's words changed Hannah's perception of her present reality?

AS

Start with me

Shout for joy, you heavens; rejoice, you earth; burst into song, you mountains! For the Lord comforts his people and will have compassion on his afflicted ones.

Many of the prophetic words in the Bible that stimulate hope in the heart and stir up God's people to action have salvation as their underlying theme. The prophets who spoke them were not only speaking into their own situation, to people who were suffering in exile from the promised land, but to all humanity throughout history, concerning the salvation from slavery to sin that God was going to perform through the life, death and resurrection of Jesus. When the Lord announces salvation, he has the power and authority that enable his words to speak that new reality into being.

Recently, searching the Internet for images for some PowerPoint presentations, I have come across some graphic scenes that have made my heart weep: starving children being stalked by vultures, young children and old men horribly maimed by war. I read Isaiah 49:9–10 and I ask why I can't perceive the salvation that the Lord has spoken into existence (Isaiah 43:19: 'Do you not perceive it?'). Then I have to stop and remember that the new reality that God speaks into being centres on the transformation he makes in human hearts through Jesus' death on the cross, and our personal response.

'We can stand on the banks of the river and rearrange the debris. We can stand on the banks of the river and rage against God as another wave of injustice washes up yet more broken pieces of humanity. To do justice, to love kindness and to walk humbly with our God is to be carried way upstream to the very source of all our suffering and there close up the ingress of our own pollution' *(Andrew Williams)*—by allowing God's new reality to be created in us through Christ and taking his compassion out into the world.

....

The kingdom of heaven is made visible on earth one soul at a time, although it already exists in all its perfection in God.

Read Micah 6:6–8: What do you need to bring to the cross to make these verses a reality in your life?

AS

Speak through me

He made my mouth like a sharpened sword, in the shadow of his hand he hid me; he made me into a polished arrow and concealed me in his quiver.

During the course of my studies, I came across these verses in an old Norwegian devotional book. They form the lectionary reading for the Sunday celebrated as the Feast of John the Baptist. They hadn't really made much impact on me before, but the writer of the book commented that these words 'certainly can be interpreted as being fulfilled by Christ and by John the Baptist, but, as Christ has already fulfilled them, and, as they are fulfilled in Christ and John, *so must they also be fulfilled in us*—for the branch is of the same substance as the tree, and the servant like his (or her) master.'

What does that mean? It is saying that although most biblical prophecy finds its ultimate fulfilment in some historical event in the past and ultimately in the life and work of Christ, these words can and must be fulfilled in us because we are children of God through Jesus' death and resurrection.

In other words, we are to allow the Lord to make our mouths 'like sharpened swords' that are moulded to fit perfectly into his ultimate purposes. And the words that the Lord charges us to speak will be like 'polished arrows' that hit the target he has picked out. If you are anything like me, speaking out is not something you relish, but we do not have a choice. Isaiah 49:1 says, 'Before I was born the Lord called me; from my birth he has made mention of my name.' Although this is usually taken to be talking about Jesus, it is also talking about all of us. It is no accident that the Lord found us and drew us to him. He has called us to speak out and change the world.

....

Invite God to fulfil his promise in your life this week.

Read Numbers 11:29. Why do you think Moses wishes that all God's people were prophets, with his Spirit in them?

AS

Fire in my bones

His word is in my heart like a fire, a fire shut up in my bones. I am weary of holding it in; indeed, I cannot.

Speaking out on behalf of God is not easy, but when the Lord pours his Spirit into our hearts to such an overwhelming degree that we have a spiritually ignited compassion for the lost, we find that we can't keep quiet. Like Jeremiah, the burden the Spirit lays on us can overpower us, and, like John Wesley, if we allow God to set our words on fire, people will come and watch us burn—that is, they will come and listen to what we are saying. That said, people will not necessarily react positively to God's message, even if it is a message of hope. It never ceases to surprise me how cynical some people can be, even when they are being given good news and the opportunity to change their life situation for the better.

Like Jeremiah, we can end up finding ourselves saying, 'The word of the Lord has brought me insult and reproach all day long' (v. 8). However, that is the nature of things with prophets, or those who speak out God's word. People feel that they have a perfect right to metaphorically 'shoot the messenger'—so much so that, over the centuries, personal suffering, both physical and mental, has become recognized as the mark of a 'true' prophet.

If you are intent on letting the Lord speak through you, don't necessarily expect it to be an easy ride, but commit your cause to the Lord (v. 12), so that your 'persecutors will… not prevail' (v. 11). One thing to remember is that even if a prophetic message is rejected by those who hear it, the validity and creational power of the message is not nullified: God's word never loses its power, nor is it ever wasted.

....

Lord, I am not ready to count and pay the cost of being willing to speak out your hope to others. Overwhelm me, so that no price is insurmountable.

AS

Words need a response

Do not trust in deceptive words… If you really change your ways… then I will let you live in… the land I gave to your ancestors for ever and ever.

I hope that over the last two weeks I have not taken too much of a scattergun approach to a large and complicated subject—the empowering nature of prophecy and how it can change reality. Even if it has left you with a bundle of questions, I hope it has put you in a position to want to find some of the answers for yourself.

I want to end this series by focusing on these verses from Jeremiah 7. There are many so-called 'prophetic' voices in secular society today, some of them calling us to change our lives in the cause of very noble ends. There are also many deceptive 'prophetic' voices out there, proclaiming messages and ideals that do not match up to the kind of life we are called to live in Christ. We need to learn to distinguish between what is worth retaining and what is necessary to discard. The same goes for the many prophetic voices within the church: there is a need to 'discern the spirits' and examine the motivation and intention behind some of the 'messages of the moment' in the church today.

There is nothing as deceitful as the human heart (Jeremiah 17:9) and it is easy to be taken in if we do not think and pray through issues carefully in the light of God's word. We must not trust deceptive words or the apparent 'truth' and immutability of our traditions, but change our ways—that is, 'deal with each other justly… not oppress the foreigner, the fatherless or the widow… not shed innocent blood… not follow other gods to [our] own harm'. Those living such a prophetic lifestyle are guaranteed to inherit God's promise.

....

Just as we have been approved by God to be entrusted with the gospel, so we speak, not to please man, but to please God who tests our hearts (1 Thessalonians 3:2–5, ESV).

AS

Do you remember Jamie Oliver's school meals campaign? There's an example of what Alie Stibbe has been writing about. Jamie's 'prophetic' call challenged the status quo in the shape of 'turkey twizzlers' with their high fat content and low nutritional value. In criticizing the nation's school meals, he also pointed to a new way forward—and he was given the authority to make changes. But his prophetic call lacked the 'energizing' element that Alie has been writing about. Will power is not enough. Legislation doesn't make the difference. Even cooking alongside school dinner ladies wasn't sufficient to change the eating habits of the nation's children. Once Jamie's changes were implemented, children voted with their feet in droves. The number of children buying those healthy school lunches plummeted.

Have you noticed how the Government is continually making new laws aimed at improving the lot of children and families in Britain? Whatever your political persuasion, you can't fail to realize that laws make little difference. No matter how many reports highlight the plight of Britain's children, criticizing the status quo and calling for changes; no matter how many laws are passed to keep children in education longer or to limit access to drink, drugs or weapons, real change happens only when hearts are changed.

Jesus' disciple Peter is one example of a man whose heart was changed. He reached a turning point in his life when he responded to Jesus' words: 'Simon Peter, do you love me?' With three simple, very similar questions, Jesus challenged Peter at his point of failure. The words 'Feed my lambs' were the prophetic energizing that Peter needed. Jesus had the authority to give him this new task and, within a few days, Peter received the Holy Spirit's power at Pentecost, which enabled him to fulfil Christ's commission. He was transformed, almost overnight. The rough, impetuous fisherman became a founding leader of the Church, with a special pastoral role—feeding Christ's sheep, making sure the first Christians were fed the good food of God's word.

Over the next fortnight, Christine Platt will be leading us through Peter's letters to those early Christians—helping us to feed on God's word, just as Christians through the ages have done. Allow Peter's practical teaching to challenge you as you invite God to transform your life.

Golden faith

You may have had to suffer grief in all kinds of trials. These have come so that your faith… may be proved genuine and may result in praise, glory and honour when Jesus Christ is revealed.

You can barely recognize foot-in-the-mouth Peter when you read this letter. Eugene Peterson remarks that with his powerful personality Peter had 'all the makings of a bully… (and religious bullies are the worst kind)' (Introduction to 1 and 2 Peter in *THE MESSAGE*).

Peter became a hugely influential leader in the early Church, but in this letter he focuses the attention of his readers not on himself but on the majesty and supremacy of Jesus. Like John the Baptist before him, his determination is that '[Jesus] must become greater; I must become less' (John 3:30). Rather than writing as a mighty leader, aiming to impress or dominate, he demonstrates the compassionate heart of a pastor. The members of his flock are under pressure and he wants to encourage and build them up. He is a testimony to the transforming power of God.

Peter writes to followers of Jesus scattered all over Asia Minor (present-day Turkey), most of whom have had a rough time. There was outright persecution. Many had lost possessions, homes and families. How do you go about encouraging someone who's going through suffering? Do you have a pity-party with them or try to jolly them along? Let's learn from Peter.

He makes no attempt to minimize the suffering. He acknowledges that it's real and it hurts. But he gives two stunning reasons to hang in there. Firstly, the suffering isn't random or pointless. As we cling on to God, our faith will grow strong and shine like gold (v. 7). Secondly, suffering will not go on for ever. Jesus is coming back, and 'golden faith' will bring him honour on that tumultuous day. When we see him face to face, we'll be so glad we persevered.

....

Lord, I come to you with my present suffering. I trust you with this pain and I invite you to make my faith like gold.

Read 1 Samuel 1 to see an example of faith growing through longstanding suffering.

CP

Like Father, like daughter

As obedient children, let yourselves be pulled into a way of life shaped by God's life, a life energetic and blazing with holiness. God said, 'I am holy; you be holy.'

I had that sobering shock some years ago when I looked in the mirror and saw my mother's face looking back at me! My youthful complexion had somehow disappeared and the familiar wrinkles predominated. The gene mixture predestined me towards a significant family resemblance. I'm grateful it wasn't my dad's face looking back—he ended up virtually bald!

How close is your resemblance to your spiritual parent? Is God's call for holiness in his children a hopeless dream—an arduous climb up an impossible mountain? How can we really be holy?

Peter reminds us that God has already made us holy. We have been redeemed and made pure by Christ's precious blood (v. 18). So, when God looks at us, he sees us through our Lord Jesus. He sees beloved holy daughters, holy like himself, set apart for him. Wow!

There is the state of being holy and also the practice of holiness. When I started my nurse training, I put on my uniform with immense pride that first day—starched cap and apron in those days. To the patients I was a nurse, but I hadn't a clue what I was doing. It was scary! I needed three years of theory and practice to become what my uniform said I was.

Because of Jesus, we have the incredible privilege of already being holy. Our mission here on earth is to live towards that, so that our lives increasingly reflect our status. We will, no doubt, make mistakes and really blow it at times, as we are human, but God promises to forgive us when we repent and to reinstate us on the path of holiness.

....

Father God, I praise you that you see me as a holy woman. Help me to live today in a way that honours you.

Read Psalm 51 to see a good response to disastrous failure.

CP

Self-image makeover

But you are a chosen people, a royal priesthood, a holy nation, a people belonging to God, that you may declare the praises of him who called you out of darkness into his wonderful light. Once you were not a people, but now you are the people of God.

Peter piles up the impressive status words. It's as if he is saying, 'Please, please recognize how special you are in God!' You are chosen. You are a royal priest. You are holy. You belong to God. At one time you were an outcast; now you are fully accepted as a valued member of God's family. There is no place for a low self-image here, but at times we forget or don't even believe how privileged we are.

It reminds me of the day Lady Diana Spencer got married. She went into the church a nursery assistant and came out a princess. How could she make that transition in her mind and grasp her new position? Some things would have helped her. She had daily reminders of her royal status. People addressed her as a princess and expected her to carry out the role of a princess. She also had access to the royal coffers.

Unfortunately, the world around us does not recognize how wonderfully privileged God's people are. No one calls us 'princess' or 'holy'. We can end up feeling ordinary or even substandard.

To combat this, we need to remind ourselves who we are in God, so that our minds and our self-image are informed by what God says and not by the opinions of the unbelieving world. As we grow in conviction of who we are in God, we will reflect beauty, joy and confidence to those around us. This is part of what it means to 'declare the praises of him who called us'. We are infinitely more privileged than Princess Diana: we have access to all the resources of heaven to help us.

Memorize and meditate on the words of our passage printed above, so that these truths come quickly to mind when your self-image is battered.

CP

Thank God for dragons

Servants, be good servants to your masters—not just to good masters, but also to bad ones. What counts is that you put up with it for God's sake when you're treated badly for no reason… This is the kind of life you've been invited into, the life Christ lived.

I am now in the enviable position of being semi-retired. I've had a variety of bosses in my working life. Some have been dragons, some angels in disguise, but the uncomfortable biblical instruction is that all bosses come under the heading of 'God-given', and I'm required to treat them all with respect and the honour due to their position. Whoops!

As I look back, I recognize that some of the most dragonish bosses were the ones I learned most from—usually about how not to be. They were also the ones who challenged my convictions with regard to ethics and honesty. They revealed my acute need to grow in patience and tolerance, as I was often tempted to let them know in no uncertain terms what a complete pain they were. 'Give thanks in all circumstances' (1 Thessalonians 5:18) became a sanity-saving motto.

The authorities mistreated Jesus abominably, inflicting humiliation, pain, injustice and a cruel death, and he silently submitted to it all, 'content to let God set things right' (v. 23b). Does this mean that we should not question any directive of any human authority, but just allow them to use or abuse us at will? I don't think so.

Jesus knew that what was happening to him was the will of his Father. There was no other way to win our freedom. In this world of ours, we have laws to protect us and we are to stand up for justice, but if we find ourselves with a 'bad master' and can do nothing to change the situation, then we have to accept that God has lessons to teach us through this time. As I look back, I'm actually grateful to the dragons. They motivated me to pursue God with renewed intensity.

....

Father, help me respect the authority figures you've placed in my life. I want to trust you to set things right in your good time.

CP

Beautiful inside and out

Don't depend on things like fancy hair styles or gold jewellery or expensive clothes to make you look beautiful. Be beautiful in your heart by being gentle and quiet. This kind of beauty will last, and God considers it very special.

As a young Christian, I went through an ascetic phase—no make-up, no jewellery, clothes that blended into the background. Fortunately, that didn't last. I realized that a dowdy frump is not an attractive demonstration of Jesus and the abundant life he offers. As one male friend commented, 'Any old barn door looks better with a coat of paint.'

I guess it's all a matter of perspective. Do I pay as much attention to my inner life as I do to outward appearance? Am I as concerned to have a pure thought life as I am to cleanse and tone my complexion? Am I working as hard at keeping my speech free from gossip and criticism as I am at flossing and brushing my pearly whites? Am I as motivated to use my hands and feet in God's service as I am to do pedicures and manicures? Do I watch what goes into my mind as intensely as I count the calories that go into my tummy? And so the list goes on.

Our bodies are a precious gift and need careful maintenance if they are to last the distance well, and it honours the giver if we make the best of what we've been given. But our bodies are only to serve us here on earth. Praise God, we get a new one in heaven! Our spirit is the immortal part of us, and beauty that is forged there brings joy to God's heart. He is thrilled when he sees precious jewels of peace, joy and patience glittering in our inner being.

Some of us wish we could have a dose of airbrushing before we face the world each day, but, insists Peter, inner beauty is what gets you noticed. It can even persuade unbelieving husbands to turn to God (vv. 1–2).

Consider your inner and exterior selves. What adjustments do you need to make to ensure that both are growing in beauty?

CP

Jesus—take the wheel

Honour Christ and let him be the Lord of your life. Always be ready to give an answer when someone asks you about your hope. Give a kind and respectful answer.

The centrepiece of this passage is verse 18—the innocent Christ died for the guilty and was raised to life—the gospel in a nutshell. Surrounding that key verse are various implications of which it means to be a Christ-follower.

Number One is that we welcome Jesus to be Lord in our life, giving him the driving seat. I'm enjoying growing older because I have so much to look back on. There were times when I thought, 'What in the world is God doing? Why? Why? Why?' Now I understand: hindsight is a marvellous thing. I see life now as a multicoloured tapestry rather than isolated threads that make no sense on their own. I recognize how God is using past experiences and weaving them into a pattern that's uniquely me. I cringe in shame when I remember trying to wrestle that steering wheel out of his grip because I thought I knew best. Other times, I continued on the journey with him but without much joy or hope for a good outcome, rather like a sulky child. Yuck!

Another implication of being a Christ-follower is that we talk about him with others—always having a positive, helpful response when people ask what we're up to. On one memorable occasion, an acquaintance enquired, 'What are you doing tonight?' Caught on the hop, I answered, 'I've got an elders' meeting and we're going over the church finances.' My voice said it all: boring! I kicked myself afterwards. I could have said, 'I'm meeting with some leaders at church to work on setting up a centre for troubled young people.' That was also on the agenda, and it would have been much more motivating and appealing.

The third challenge is that we should 'treat everyone with kindness'—even difficult people (vv. 8–9).

....

Lord Jesus, what a privilege it is to be yours. Help me to honour you today in the way I live. Give me opportunities to talk about you.

CP

71

The end is nigh

Everything will soon come to an end. So be serious and be sensible enough to pray. Most important of all, you must sincerely love each other, because love wipes away many sins. Welcome people into your home… use your gift well… bring honour to God.

Last night, here in New Zealand, we experienced a lunar eclipse. I peered at the menacing black shadow encroaching on the moon's brightness. The sight sent shivers down my spine. Later in the process, the moon appeared reddish. It reminded me of Joel's prophecy that the moon would turn to blood as a sign that the Lord will soon return (2:31). I thought, 'Wow, he could come back tonight!'

How do you respond to the prospect of meeting the mighty Lord Jesus in his power and glory? For me, it was a wake-up call, a time to refocus my mind and sort out priorities. If I truly believed he was coming today, this week, this month, how would I live?

Peter urges us to be ready to suffer (v. 1), to steer well clear of sin (v. 2), to pray (v. 7), to love others (v. 8), to be hospitable (v. 9), and to use our gifts to the full (v. 10).

Scripture gives many reminders that Jesus is coming back. 'The judge is just outside the door,' says James 5:9. Jesus himself told the parables of the ten bridesmaids (Matthew 25:1–13) and the watchful servants (Mark 13:32–37). His return is now nearly 2000 years nearer than when he spoke these parables.

His coming will be unexpected. He is not going to send a quick email or text message to warn us. It is his wish that we remain on the alert, ready to welcome him at any moment. Are you ready? Am I ready? I would hate to have regrets in my heart when I look on that glorious face. I would want to have a spotless conscience and be able to bow at his feet knowing that all was well between us.

....

Jesus, thank you for life. I want to make the most of every day you give me, conscious that it may be my last.

Read Mark 13 to see what Jesus taught about the end times.

CP

The upside of suffering

Friends, when life gets really difficult, don't jump to the conclusion that God isn't on the job... This is a spiritual refining process... So if you find life difficult because you're doing what God said, take it in stride. Trust him.

I was recently at a conference where one of the speakers likened God to her own father, whom she could twist around her little finger. She was attempting to communicate to 200 teenage girls how much God loved them and how precious they were to him. Great stuff—they need to know that in order to have a chance to build a healthy self-esteem in today's appearance-obsessed world.

However, I was uncomfortable with the lack of balance. Mighty God is not a celestial Father Christmas, ready to give us anything we want. If Peter's readers had received that type of teaching, they would have stumbled at the first glimpse of persecution. We only have to look at Jesus' life to know that suffering is part of following him. God doesn't want spoiled brats; he wants holy children. The spiritual refining process is a necessary part of Christian maturity. Even mighty Moses and daring David received discipline when they fell short of God's standard. They were forgiven but had to live with the consequences of their actions.

As a caring father, God can't let us get away with murder. He has to discipline us when we do wrong, but he also allows suffering to come into our lives to grow spiritual fruit. How often I have prayed for patience, and then been surprised and a bit cross when God brought an infuriating individual into my life so that he could answer my prayer and grow patience within me!

The persecution we face may be minuscule in comparison with that suffered by Peter's readers, but, whatever circumstances we meet, whether God's discipline for wrongdoing or his spiritual refining, we need not be surprised but aim to 'take it in stride' and 'trust him'.

....

As you share your faith journey with younger Christians, do you equip them to face suffering with the right attitude?

CP

73

Shepherds required

Be shepherds of God's flock that is under your care, serving as overseers—not because you must, but because you are willing, as God wants you to be; not greedy for money, but eager to serve; not lording it over those entrusted to you, but being examples to the flock.

I recently hit a crossroads in my life and sought God for guidance for my next phase. His words 'Feed my sheep' came to me, which reminded me of Jesus' recommissioning of Peter in John 21:15–17, after his threefold denial of Christ.

The command 'Feed my sheep' must have been deeply engraved in Peter's mind and spirit. In his broken state of failure, the words would have been like a drenching, restorative waterfall, sluicing away the dark feelings of guilt and inspiring hope for the future. Peter accepted Jesus' forgiveness and was able to put the past behind him. He embraced his new role and became a dynamic, compassionate shepherd of God's flock. In this letter he pleads with leaders to be wise, careful and loving shepherds, keeping the welfare of the flock as highest priority. He warns them that the enemy of souls is close by (vv. 8–9), but reassures them that God is mightier than the enemy (v. 11).

When Jesus reinstated Peter, he warned him that suffering and death would come to him (John 21:18–19). Peter knew that his days were numbered. He was determined to do his utmost, while he still had breath, to ensure that God's people were fed, protected and led into good paths.

It's newborn lamb season here in New Zealand. They are so cute—small blobs of fluffy white fun! Each one sticks close to its mum and looks to her to see how to manage life. In God's economy, a shepherd can have a small flock or a large one. This instruction isn't only for pastors. God invites all of us to play our part in caring for 'lambs'. Whether you have one or 100 lambs to nurture, they are a sacred responsibility.

....

Whom are you nurturing? How can you be more of an encouragement and a positive example to them?

Paul shares his own example of godly shepherding in 1 Thessalonians 2:1–20.

CP

Healthy soul nutrition

If you keep growing in this way, it will show that what you know about our Lord Jesus Christ has made your lives useful and meaningful. But if you don't grow, you are like someone who is nearsighted or blind, and you have forgotten that your past sins are forgiven.

I love spring! There are buds bursting with potential, birds busy with homemaking, and growth sprouting out all over. Consistent, obvious, continued growth is an imperative in God's natural world, but also, insists Peter in his second letter, it's an imperative in the spiritual realm. Standing still is not an option. If we stand still, we will stagnate. Lack of growth shows we have forgotten that we have been forgiven for our past sins. Peter is echoing Paul's words: 'If anyone is in Christ, the new creation has come: the old has gone, the new is here!' (2 Corinthians 5:17, TNIV). New creations need to grow and reflect their Creator.

To ensure growth, Peter urges his readers to aim at goodness, understanding, self-control, patience, devotion to God, concern for others and love (vv. 5–6). It's quite a list! I find these qualities hard to assess on a daily basis. Sometimes my concern for others is high, other times lamentably low. I find it useful to remember that just as plants need rain, sun and nutrients from the earth in order to grow, so my relationship with God also needs feeding. God's word is our essential food. As we read God's word, pray over what he says (just as you are doing in setting aside time to focus on these notes) and then do what he says (James 1:22), we will grow.

So, rather than navel-gaze about how much I'm loving or not loving others, I choose to focus on my relationship with Jesus, making sure that my priority is to read and study God's word, and that I aim to please him every day. He, by his Spirit, will cause his beautiful fruit (Galatians 5:22–23) to become more evident in my life. Growth will happen. How fantastic is that?

....

Father God, draw me nearer to your wonderful self and make me more like Jesus as I feed on your word.

CP

It's true!

We were eyewitnesses of his majesty. He received honour and glory from God the Father when the voice came to him from the Majestic Glory, saying, 'This is my Son, whom I love; with him I am well pleased.'

Peter is alarmed! False teachers have invaded the church and are confusing the believers. His pastoral heart is churning. How can he protect the flock against this threat? It is especially urgent as he knows that his time is short (v. 14). (He was martyred a few years after writing this letter.) He decides to refer the church back to the truth of scripture and his own eyewitness account of Jesus' life and transfiguration. These, he says, are the proofs I've staked my life on.

Peter, with James and John, had the astounding privilege of seeing Jesus transfigured as the heavenly king that he truly is (Matthew 17:1–8). When Jesus was transformed on the mountain, God spoke clearly to them and they saw the Old Testament heavyweights, Moses and Elijah, talking with Jesus. But, compelling though his testimony is, Peter realizes that his readers have no such experience to look back on, so he reminds them of the integrity and trustworthiness of scripture. The false teachers were bringing in their own version of reality, whereas in scripture we have God's version. In contrast to the false teachers, scripture is divinely inspired, not human-inspired (vv. 20–21).

If Peter were here today, he would say the same thing to us. The Western world has been heavily influenced by postmodern thinking, so that people construct their own 'truth' and no absolutes are accepted. Consequently many people are rudderless, lost in a maze of gobbledygook. 'Base your life on God's word,' Peter would say. 'It's the only reliable source of truth.' Peter gave his testimony. We, too, have a testimony to share with those around us. We also have scripture as our gold standard in matters of truth.

Think about ways you can share your experiences of walking with God, and his word, with those around you.

CP

Vulnerability

These people are springs without water and mists driven by a storm. Blackest darkness is reserved for them. For they mouth empty, boastful words and, by appealing to the lustful desires of sinful human nature, they entice people who are just escaping from those who live in error.

In the primary school where I teach Values, there is a unit for children with special needs. One day a farmer brought in a newborn calf for the children to see and touch. The calf and the children were excited and skittish. There was a watchful posse of teachers, parents and farmer hovering around the group to make sure these especially vulnerable children and the animal came to no harm. We all recognized the potential for accidents and took appropriate steps to minimize danger.

Peter warns that false teachers target the vulnerable, especially those who've just escaped from darkness and come into the light 'from the power of Satan to God' (Acts 26:18). This is a precarious time in a believer's life, when there is a danger of being led down wrong paths. I thank God for those who discipled me when I was an impressionable raw convert. They helped me build a solid foundation for my walk with God. Now, as a mature believer, I still need to be alert to recognize and refute any teaching contrary to scripture. False teachers are definitely out there and also, sadly, within our churches.

This chapter contains dire warnings for false teachers and for God's people. False teachers promise much but deliver little. From a distance they may look inviting but there is no refreshment to be found there. We need to guard against persuasive personalities who 'mouth empty, boastful words.' Discerning watchwomen are needed.

None of us at the school would have dreamt of leaving those special needs children and the calf on their own. Yet how many spiritual babies are abandoned at birth—prey to every negative influence?

....

Holy Spirit of truth, grant me the discernment to identify false teaching. Help me also to play my part in protecting young believers from harm.

CP

Too late

God has commanded the present heavens and earth to remain until the day of judgment. Then they will be set on fire, and ungodly people will be destroyed… God is patient, because he wants everyone to turn from sin and no one to be lost. The day of the Lord's return will surprise us.

'Strike me dead, God, if you're there!' Jeff's violent challenge felt like a physical blow and my heart turned to ice. His outburst came in response to my fumbling attempts to explain the reality of God to him. I silently pleaded, 'God, please don't answer that prayer.' (He didn't.)

There were scoffers in Peter's time and there are scoffers now. People who say, 'If God is who he says he is, let him *do* something; let him show himself' choose to forget that he has already displayed his power in judgment. The flood in Noah's time destroyed all life, except those hidden safely in the ark.

Final judgment will come, suddenly and unexpectedly, just as it did for Noah's contemporaries. We can imagine that they recognized their error too late and begged in panic for Noah to open the door of the ark, not realizing that God was the one who had closed the door (Genesis 7:16). Noah could do no more for them. Perhaps he had warned them and they had scoffed at his warnings. Their last sight before they succumbed to the waves would have been the ark sailing out of reach. Flashing through their minds would have been all the missed opportunities they'd had to repent and turn to God.

To my knowledge, Jeff still isn't ready to confront his maker. He is mellowing but has not yet bowed the knee. God is showing great patience towards him, but neither he nor I can presume on that patience for ever. Judgment will come. This spurs me on to pray for Jeff with renewed urgency. I long for Jesus' return in majestic glory, and yet dread it at the same time. So many friends and relatives will be lost for ever.

....

Mighty Saviour, open the hearts and minds of my friends and family to respond to your invitation to escape judgment and receive new life.

CP

Today's the day

You ought to live holy and godly lives as you look forward to the day of God and speed its coming… Make every effort to be found spotless, blameless and at peace with him.

My niece got married last summer. For months before the big occasion she followed a strict beauty routine: healthy diet, vigorous exercise, skin-cleansing, hair-conditioning, nail-shaping. Her whole life and routine and all her decision-making revolved around preparing for this special event, all to ensure that she looked fabulous for the day—and she did.

Peter says that the Lord's return should be our daily motivation to live lives that please God, so that we are ready and prepared to meet him face to face with no shame or regrets.

The wedding photos attest to my niece's diligence in following her self-imposed regime. Her hair shone, her skin bloomed, her body was toned and shapely, her nails the epitome of femininity. She had a specific date to aim for, whereas none of us knows the date of Jesus' return (Matthew 24:36), so we need to be in a state of high alert, ready every day.

Today the news bulletin told of another devastating earthquake in Indonesia. Life as we know it is fragile and transient (Psalm 103:15–16). There are no guarantees for tomorrow. This moment is all we can be sure of, so let's live it to the full, for the glory of God. That involves dealing with sin quickly, as soon as we're aware of it, and saying sorry to the people affected, if appropriate. It also involves a daily consecration of our lives to God—encompassing the use of our time, our gifts, our finances, our planning and decisions, and our leisure activities.

Why not try a morning prayer like this? 'Lord, may your kingdom come soon. May your will be done in my life today. I submit to your loving guidance and intervention and want to live to honour you.'

....

If you knew that Jesus was coming back tomorrow, what changes would you make in your life?

CP

What life-changing experiences have you had? For some, a sudden boost or drop in finances forces change. Others are confronted by illness or redundancy. Children make changes to couples' lives, for better and sometimes for worse. Bereavement makes changes to everyone's lives.

Most changes creep up on us gradually but some are sudden and bring the added challenge of adjusting to new circumstances. Peter's life was transformed by Jesus' invitation to 'follow me'. The fisherman left his nets and became a follower of Jesus. That change was consolidated by three years of working and living alongside Jesus. As a result, Peter recognized that this was 'the Messiah, the Son of the living God' (Matthew 16:16, TNIV). Peter was also one of the privileged few who saw Jesus transfigured—literally shining in the light of the glory of God (Matthew 17). But even with all that life-transforming evidence, Peter abandoned his Saviour to the cross and denied that he ever knew him. Thankfully, God delights to use people who have no human qualifications—especially those who have disqualified themselves. The Bible is full of evidence that God 'gives grace to the humble'.

Moses is another example, as Jennifer Rees Larcombe will be showing us over the next two weeks. Moses' life changed while he was still a baby. Born a slave's son, he was transformed into a prince when an Egyptian princess rescued him. But with one impetuous act his life was transformed again: a murderer on the run, he left palace life for a shepherd's job in the desert. Forty years later, he was so humble, he felt unable to fulfil the task for which he was uniquely qualified. Although he had been rejected by his people and his adoptive family, he had not been abandoned by God. In fact, God was his friend and trainer through four decades of wilderness training.

Every life has highs and lows, and often it is in the tough times that we learn the most about ourselves and our God. Moses' training prepared him to negotiate his people's release from Eqypt and lead them to the promised land. Peter's training equipped him to lead the Church, preparing Christ's radiant bride. As you reflect on your own life, how is God training you? If life seems tough, ask God for his special gift of grace and an awareness of his love to see you through.

The 'hands off' mother

At that time Moses was born—a beautiful child in God's eyes. His parents cared for him at home for three months. When they had to abandon him, Pharaoh's daughter adopted him and raised him as her own son.

For the next couple of weeks we'll be looking at one of my favourite Bible characters. I seem to identify with him in so many ways and perhaps you will, too. Today we remember the brave heroes who fought for our freedom in two World Wars. Moses felt anything but brave or heroic, yet he did one of the most courageous and difficult jobs of all time.

Let's start by setting the scene. For 370 years the descendents of Jacob had been enjoying a prosperous life as sheep farmers in the fertile Nile delta. Pharaoh had given them Egypt's 'best land' (Genesis 45:18) out of gratitude to Joseph, who had saved Egypt from famine by his brilliant administrative strategies.

When a new dynasty seized power, Joseph became forgotten history and the new Pharaoh fancied the Israelites' lush location as a site for a new city and royal residence. He also realized that two million Jews could be either a national threat or a cheap, readymade workforce for his building projects.

In spite of Pharaoh's programme of forced labour and near starvation, a baby boom scared him into culling all newborn baby boys.

How awful for Moses' mother to realize she was pregnant but to know that if her baby was a boy he would be seized and drowned (Exodus 1:22). Yet when she held him in her arms she just knew that God was going to protect him (Hebrews 11:23), because he was 'beautiful… in God's eyes (Acts 7:20, NLT). For three months she hid him; then, obeying Pharaoh, she placed him in the Nile, leaving the rest to God.

....

Is God asking you to stand back and leave him to protect someone you are worried about—as Moses' mother did?

If this story intrigues you, enjoy the fuller version in Exodus 1:8—2:3.

JRL

God's school

When the princess saw the basket among the reeds, she sent her maid to get it for her. When the princess opened it, she saw the baby. The little boy was crying, and she felt sorry for him.

Strange? A royal princess adopting a foreign baby on impulse? But suppose she had been burning with indignation at her father's cruel edict? When I hear about natural disasters and injustice, I always long to help, but I think, 'What difference could the efforts of one individual make?' so I end up doing nothing!

A freak high tide had landed thousands of starfish on a beach, then receded, leaving them to die in the hot sun. A man saw a child desperately throwing starfish back into the sea, one by one. 'What difference can your efforts possibly make?' he asked. As the child hurled the next starfish into the sea she replied, 'A lot of difference to this one!'

Perhaps the princess, knowing she could do nothing to save all those babies, decided that she could, at least, make a difference to one. By doing so, she ultimately saved an entire nation. Jesus multiplied a child's picnic lunch to feed five thousand, so there is no knowing what he will do with an urgent prayer, small action or donation.

Pharaoh had many harems all over Egypt and it was not uncommon for foreign children to be brought up and educated with his own numerous offspring. There are records of royal foster children going on to occupy high-ranking positions in Egypt. The man God was preparing to free a horde of slaves and turn them into a nation would need a first-class education if he was going to understand and record for posterity God's blueprint for his people's legal system (Deuteronomy 31:24). God has wonderful plans for each of our lives (Jeremiah 29:11) and he wants to use everything that happens to us, good and bad, to prepare us for our future destiny.

....

Lord, you know the situations and the people that I am finding difficult right now, but I give you permission to use this mess for your glory.

JRL

Life begins at 40

The Israelites groaned in their slavery and cried out, and their cry for help because of their slavery went up to God.

Life ended at 40 for Moses—at least, his comfortable, privileged life as an Egyptian prince did. Acts 7:22–23 tells us that, by the age of 40, he had been 'educated in all the wisdom of the Egyptians and was powerful in speech and action'. His trained mind and military prowess had probably landed him a plum job in a government department. Life was great; he looked and acted like an Egyptian (Exodus 2:19) and kept well away from his Jewish relatives. Then, mysteriously, he changed (Hebrews 11:24–25). A belated desire to help his people sent him off to make a systematic inspection of their working conditions. Defending an unpopular ethnic minority was a risky thing for him to do (see Pharaoh's furious reaction in Exodus 2:15) and it shows that Moses had experienced a massive shift in the way he thought about his own identity and purpose in life.

Whenever God wants to move me into a deeper relationship with himself or a new sphere of service, he has a way of making me feel suddenly discontented with my life, which previously I have found safe and satisfying. Have you ever felt 'stirred up' by God?

On paper, Moses was perfectly qualified for the job of freeing the slaves, so he set off, brimming with self-confidence, casting himself in the role of 'rescuer'. Unfortunately, he went in his own strength and doesn't appear to have prayed about his venture. God cannot use people who rely on their own high-quality gifts and qualifications, because they have so much going for them in terms of natural ability that they feel they have no need of God's help.

Moses' self-motivated mission failed utterly; God needed to teach him to trust him alone before Moses would be any use at all. Have you ever had your self-confidence shredded by circumstances? I have! I had to exchange self-confidence for God-confidence, just as Moses did.

....

Someone once said to me that the only qualification any of us needs to serve God is to know our own utter inadequacy and God's total adequacy.

JRL

Profitable investment

Now Moses was tending the flock of Jethro his father-in-law, the priest of Midian, and he led the flock to the far side of the wilderness and came to Horeb, the mountain of God. There the angel of the Lord appeared to him in flames of fire.

Moses must have felt as desolate as his surroundings. His instinctive action in helping seven damsels in distress (2:16–17) led him to the home of a local chieftain, but his marriage to one of the girls does not appear to have been very successful. As Moses followed his father-in-law's scrawny sheep around the wilderness, he obviously felt like an alien (2:22) and a failure, because shepherding was considered the lowest job of all by Egyptians. However, God knew exactly what he was doing! As an Egyptian prince, Moses could never have led the Israelites through that desert. It takes years of experience and local knowledge to survive out there—and that was exactly what Moses was acquiring.

I always wanted to do something special for God but, when disabling illness kept me in a wheelchair for eight years, I felt at first as if God had chucked my life on the scrap heap. Then I began to realize that, in God's eyes, the things I wanted to do for him were not nearly as important as my companionship with him. God used those inactive years to change me from a mere servant into a friend. I believe that's what happened to Moses. He could have spent those lonely years wallowing in self-pity or remorse, but instead he developed the intimate relationship with God that characterized him for the rest of his life. Notice the natural way he shares his doubts and feelings with God in verses 11 and 13, talking to him as he would to a friend. He also formed the habit of always turning to God instantly when something went wrong, rather than trying to figure out a way to solve the problem himself (see 5:22–23).

Have you ever had a 'burning bush' experience, when you felt that God encountered you in a special way? Stop and savour the memory.

JRL

Facing up to fear

Then the Lord said to him, 'What is that in your hand?' 'A staff,' he replied. The Lord said, 'Throw it on the ground.'

If the Lord had told Moses to go and free the slaves 40 years before, he would have gone like a shot! Now the very idea terrifies him. While it was good that his bumptious bounce had been flattened, all he had gone through had left him timid and plagued by fear. I feel for him, because fear and worry have always been my challenges.

For years, Moses may have been haunted by the thought that Pharaoh's secret police would come after him. Or he might have dreamed he was trying to explain to those jeering slaves his desire to help, only to find that he couldn't speak. (Trauma may have left him with a speech impediment: v. 10.)

Most people of 80 (see 7:7) would relish the comfort of an arm-chair, but Moses only had his shepherd's crook to lean on. It was his comfort, but also his security—his weapon of defence. Although he may not have enjoyed life in the desert, familiarity equals comfort and security. The prison you know can feel safer than the prospect of freedom. God was asking him to throw down the symbol of his security and watch it turn into something he feared. Poisonous snakes were life-threatening: no wonder Moses ran! But God wanted to teach him to walk towards all the things that scared him, because by grasping them (v. 4) he could see God transforming them into blessings for others (vv. 5, 17).

For years, a past experience made me too afraid to do things I knew God was calling me to do. 'I'll always have this handicap,' I told myself, 'because of my childhood.' A deep experience of God's inner healing changed all that. God doesn't always remove our fear when we have to do something we are afraid to do, but he does help us to 'do it afraid'.

....

When we give our past to the Lord, it no longer has the power to spoil the present.

If fear troubles you, too, you'll find some encouraging verses in Isaiah 41:10–14.

JRL

Failure

Then Moses went back to the Lord and protested, 'Why have you brought all this trouble on your own people, Lord? Why did you send me? Ever since I came to Pharaoh as your spokesman, he has been even more brutal to your people.'

I can picture Moses marching into Pharaoh's throne room, knees knocking but chin up, sure of success because God had promised to be with him and show him what to say and do. What a huge shock to his faith when he and his brother were rapidly flung out with Pharaoh's sneering taunts ringing in their ears! The new Pharaoh was not impressed by two shabbily dressed octogenarians. He was young, arrogant and ambitious, bent on building monuments to immortalize himself. In order to do that, he needed slave labour; he was not going to give them time off to worship their 'imaginary' god. He merely saw Israelites as subhuman tools at his disposal.

Have you ever nerved yourself to do something for God, only to fail utterly? When Emma's boss enforced an office procedure that was dishonest, she prayed hard and felt that God wanted her to express her concern to the boss. His quick talk tied her in humiliating knots and left her feeling a fool. Emma was devastated and vowed she'd never do anything for God again. Then a Sunday sermon encouraged her to try again. This time the boss changed his policy—and offered Emma a promotion.

Moses must have felt like running back to the desert when he realized his interview with Pharaoh had increased his people's suffering and destroyed his initial popularity with their leaders, who were so crushed by cruelty that they wouldn't listen to him any more (4:30–32; 6:9).

In the past, when I felt that God had let me down, I stopped praying and moaned to my friends. Moses, faced with apparent disaster, turned directly to God himself, and wasn't afraid to say how disappointed he felt (5:22–23).

....

*Is God your first destination
when things go wrong? With
God, failure is never final.*

See how King David expressed
his disappointment with God,
in Psalm 22:1–11.

JRL

The battle

This is what the Lord says: by this you will know that I am the Lord: with the staff that is in my hand I will strike the water of the Nile, and it will be changed into blood. The fish in the Nile will die, and the river will stink.

The story of this year-long battle fascinates me. Pharaoh's obstinacy is phenomenal. He allowed his country to be ruined (10:7) by God's ten terrible judgments rather than admit to the inferior power of his imaginary gods. Egyptians worshipped the Nile as the source of life, but they saw it polluted—stinking with dead fish. The frog was their fertility god, but frogs soon lay in rotting heaps, powerless to prevent crops and livestock from being destroyed by hail, disease and locusts. The earth god failed to defend Egypt from gnats and flies, which caused skin infections; and Ra, their famous sun god, had no power to overcome darkness.

God was not just showing off to impress Pharaoh; he needed to raise Moses' profile in the eyes of the slaves so that they would follow him, as well as growing Moses' own shattered confidence. If you have time to read the whole story (chapters 7—13) you will find it both funny and tragic, but you'll also see how Moses grows in stature, standing firm against all Pharaoh's suggested compromises and becoming one of the greatest leaders of all time.

While destruction rained throughout Egypt, amazingly the Jewish quarter was totally unaffected. God said that it showed he didn't view his people as the Egyptians did (11:7). They considered the Jews as scum and themselves as a super-race. We all tend to value successful, beautiful, gifted people far more highly than those we consider unattractive failures. God's viewpoint is totally different. He sees the best in each of us and loves us enough to help us deal with the 'bad bits'. If only we looked at others through his spectacles!

Lord, sometimes I wonder why you don't make my life just a bit easier! Yet I know you've always grown my faith during times of conflict and upheaval.

JRL

Stepping into the impossible

Moses answered the people, 'Do not be afraid. Stand firm and you will see the deliverance the Lord will bring you today… The Lord will fight for you; you need only to be still.'

What a nightmare—trapped with your little children and old people between the sea and a rapidly advancing army! Pharaoh had changed his mind yet again. See how quickly the Israelites panicked, blaming everything on Moses (vv. 11–12). They had been born in slavery, cringing helplessly before their masters. It would take Moses the rest of his life to transform them into a free, self-respecting nation who trusted God for everything.

We were born into slavery, too. Paul calls us 'slaves of sin' (Romans 6:6). When we decided to follow Jesus, we were set free, yet we easily revert to slave-mode when something goes wrong. We feel trapped by circumstances or controlled by other people and see ourselves as powerless victims with nowhere to run. I've proved Exodus 14:14 true so many times in my life! We really can be still and know that the Lord will sort everything out for us, so long as we are willing to step out into his impossible-looking solution (v. 15).

I love the way the pillar of cloud moved (vv. 19–20). It was the visible presence and power of the Lord himself and it usually led the way, looking like a cloud in the day and a tower of flame at night. As the Egyptians came up to attack from behind, though, it moved back between them and the Israelites, looking like a wall of confusing darkness to the soldiers but comforting light to God's people. Whenever someone makes me feel intimidated or when I go into an interview or a hospital appointment, I think of this story. I ask the Lord to stand between me and the person who scares me. That way, he absorbs all the flak while I hide safely behind him. Try it the next time someone has a row with you!

....

Help me to remember that it was for freedom that you have set me free. Don't let me be daunted by anything or anyone.

To find out more about being still in the middle of turmoil, read Psalm 46.

JRI

Faith spelt R.I.S.K.

Then the Lord said to Moses, 'I am going to rain down bread from heaven for you. The people are to go out each day and gather enough for that day. In this way I will test them and see whether they will follow my instructions.'

I'm writing this in August, surrounded by bulging bags; we're holidaying in a remote area so I've planned food for every meal, clothes for all weathers and medical supplies for any emergency. Detailed preparations make me feel safe, but Moses was not allowed that luxury.

God asked him to lead two million people into the heart of the desert, which Moses knew from experience was so dry and harsh that it could scarcely provide enough food and water for just one person. It was no wonder the people were jittery (15:24). Moses didn't know how God was going to provide for all those people, but he was sure that he would. Sometimes I'm tempted to feel, 'I'll never change; at my age I'm stuck with my weaknesses.' Yet Moses changed radically at the age of 80, from someone who was full of doubts and fears into a man of rock-hard faith—so there's hope for us all!

As the people swarmed furiously round Moses, demanding water and then food, their complaints did not rattle him. He simply turned to God and asked for what they needed. It was vital that the slaves saw him doing that, because God also wanted to grow their faith. They only had a hazy knowledge of their ancestral deity, but God wanted them to know his character so intimately that they could trust and depend on him for every detail of their lives (16:4). Only then could he give them the blessings of the promised land.

Sometimes God has kept me waiting right to the last minute, but he always provides in the end. Waiting grows our faith, which is so vitally important to him (Hebrews 11:6).

....

Lord, you told your people only to collect enough manna for each day. Help me to live like that, trusting you for one day's strength at a time.

JRL

Terrifying splendour

Mount Sinai was covered with smoke, because the Lord descended on it in fire. The smoke billowed up from it like smoke from a furnace, and the whole mountain trembled violently. As the sound of the trumpet grew louder and louder, Moses spoke and the voice of God answered him.

The people must have been terrified! But God was about to make a solemn pact with them and he needed their attention (vv. 10–12). He had been showing them his love for months; now he had to demonstrate his holiness and power. They needed to fear him enough to obey him, just as we must fear the law enough to avoid breaking it.

'You live by my rules and you'll be happy and prosperous; disobey them and misery follows'—that was the deal. God wanted the rest of the world to see that living by his rules resulted in happiness and prosperity, so that they would want to know and obey him too (vv. 5–6).

Here is the recipe for happiness that he gave them (see Exodus 20). 'Everyone should be free to enjoy his own patch of land, so there's to be no coveting or stealing other people's possessions. Children need the security of two loving parents, so adultery is out—it destroys marriage. Everyone should get along happily with others, so no dishonesty or murder. To avoid family rowing and neglect of the elderly, be good to your parents. Avoid stress: take a day each week to rest and get to know me better. Don't worship images of me: relate to me direct; put me first and everything else will fall into place.'

We dismiss God's rules as negative and restricting but, actually, suffering always follows when we selfishly put our own interests before someone else's. We all break those ten rules frequently in all kinds of little ways, telling ourselves, 'God's so kind, he'll understand.' He is kind, but the story of Sinai reminds me that he's also holy.

••

We hear a lot about intimacy with God these days, but are we in danger of reducing God to a sloppy, sentimental Father Christmas figure?

JRL

The secret weapon

When the people saw that Moses was so long in coming down from the mountain, they gathered round Aaron and said, 'Come, make us gods who will go before us. As for this fellow Moses who brought us up out of Egypt, we don't know what has happened to him.'

Whenever I've had a special encounter with God or taken a big leap forward in my relationship with him, I always seem to hit a bad patch when my faith is seriously tested. The Israelites had that experience, too. Moses had returned from the mountain and given them God's Ten Commandments verbally, but when he disappeared into those terrifying clouds again for six long weeks, to receive more detailed rules, they panicked: 'Moses and his God have left us stranded! We need a new god.'

They never managed to manipulate Moses by their whinging but Aaron was soon under their thumb (vv. 2, 25). Pooling their jewellery, they created the Egyptian god Apis, symbolizing fertility and strength, then threw a party in his honour, which soon degenerated into an orgy (v. 6). God was so distressed, he felt like destroying them all, particularly Aaron (Deuteronomy 9:20), and starting again from scratch. Moses' response was amazing (vv. 11, 32): he cared about God's reputation more than personal promotion and, although he was also furious with the people, he loved them enough to stand up for them before God. He often had to do the same thing on subsequent occasions before they reached the promised land.

I'd love to be an intercessor like that! So often, when my family or friends get themselves into bad trouble, I heap them with reproaches or advice (while worrying myself ill about them). If only I remembered to take them straight to the Lord in prayer! God has placed this incredibly powerful weapon in our hands, but we just don't realize its dynamic power for our families and communities—the devil makes sure of that.

....

Lord, I want to make a difference in this world, so please make me a powerful prayer warrior.

See how Moses learnt the art of intercession, in Exodus 17:8–13.

JRL

Longing for intimacy

'If you are pleased with me, teach me your ways so I may know you and continue to find favour with you. Remember that this nation is your people.' The Lord replied, 'My Presence will go with you, and I will give you rest.' Then Moses said to him, 'If your Presence does not go with us, do not send us up from here… What else will distinguish me and your people from all the other people on the face of the earth?'

Have you ever felt as if God was far away? He promised he would never leave us (Hebrews 13:5b) but he never promised we would always feel his presence. Sometimes, when we do or say something that hurts someone else, God is displeased and, like the sun going behind a cloud, he withdraws the sense of his presence.

God spared his people after the golden calf incident because Moses interceded, but God withdrew from them, telling Moses to take the people on to the promised land without him. The idea of going without God's presence was unthinkable for Moses and the people but, once they repented, God totally forgave them.

When our relationship with the Lord feels dry and dead, we do need to ask him why. He soon shows us if we have sinned, and he forgives instantly when we repent. However, we must remember that tiredness, depression or grief can also, temporarily, rob us of spiritual joy.

The thing I long for most in life is the kind of intimacy that Moses had with God (v. 11). His desire for God was insatiable (vv. 13, 18). Some people are content to be 'pew-fillers', others are satisfied by serving God, but there are a few who are not content until they live so close to God they can hear his heartbeat—sense his thoughts, feelings and plans.

....

Lord, Moses realized that it is your presence in us that makes us different. Please may people be attracted to you today—when they see you in me.

JRL

'All in the mind'

'If the Lord is pleased with us, he will lead us into that land, a land flowing with milk and honey, and will give it to us. Only do not rebel against the Lord. And do not be afraid of the people of the land, because... the Lord is with us.'

Everyone waited eagerly for the return of the twelve spies, but only two of them described all the glorious things the Lord was about to give them. The other ten only remembered giants and fortified cities.

It is not tough situations that make us feel afraid or miserable, but what we think about those situations. One woman will see the loss of her job as an irrevocable disaster while another will view the same scenario as a challenge—a doorway to new experiences. The first feels depressed and anxious; the second feels confident and positive.

As they listened to the spies' reports, the people had a choice—to believe the bad report and feel like helpless grasshoppers or to feel inspired by believing that 'God has promised us victory!' Unfortunately, they made the wrong choice and without more intercession by Moses they would all have died on the spot. Instead, God sentenced them to 40 years in the wilderness.

There is nothing we can do that hurts God more than doubting his ability and desire to keep his promises to care for us. Feel his grief (14:11)! I've never met a Christian who didn't suffer from doubts occasionally, but we can deliberately choose to embrace them or to kick them out.

Perhaps we all have frightening giants and invincible-looking citadels in our lives—events we're dreading, people who intimidate us or problems we can't solve. When we focus on them, they seem to grow larger, but when we focus on God and his promises, we soon realize that he is so much bigger than any of them.

....

Lord, I'm sorry about my negative thinking. Please give me your courage when mine runs out.

If your thoughts control your feelings, read 2 Corinthians 10:3–5.

JRL

The final challenge

'Climb one of the mountains east of the river, and look out over the land I have given the people of Israel. After you have seen it, you will die....Then Moses said to the Lord, 'O Lord... please appoint a new man as leader for the community. Give them someone who will... lead them into battle, so the community of the Lord will not be like sheep without a shepherd.'

Critical, grumbling churches discourage or even crush their leaders. Poor Moses had 40 years of being blamed for everything and it finally got to him. He was furious when he struck that rock (20:10–11). For the first time, he felt he had to prove his personal power rather than God's glory. It is a very serious sin when we use the gifts and power that God gives us for his service to boost our own reputation with others.

In the past, Moses had successfully pleaded with God many times over, but notice how calmly he accepted this decision (27:15–16). We should never accept bad situations passively, but we do need to ask God how to pray. Perhaps God showed Moses that it was time to accept without argument. Moses' only concern was for the people (27:17).

It is not easy to hand over responsibility for something that has been important to us. Susan had run the children's work in her church most successfully for years. She was furious when the new minister wanted a younger person to take over. Two years later, she had to admit that her successor was doing an excellent job and had been blessed through the challenge. We have to hold the things we do for God in an open hand, because he may want to 'grow' someone else through doing the job.

Perhaps there was another reason for Moses' calm acceptance of approaching death. He wanted to be with the Master he loved so intimately, more than he desired to serve him by leading the people into the land.

....

Moses accomplished one of the greatest feats in history yet his epitaph simply reads, 'Moses, whom the Lord knew face to face' (Deuteronomy 34:10). Intimate friendship is God's priority.

JRL

It is intriguing to think that Moses had to wear a veil after being in God's presence: his face shone with the light of God's glory and the Israelites couldn't bear it (Exodus 34:33–35). Years later, Moses' face was shining again. This time he was in the presence of Jesus, transfigured on a mountain-top (Matthew 17:1–3).

As you spend time day by day, using these notes to help you to focus on Jesus and his word, you are probably unaware of the difference those few moments make. Radiating God's glory isn't a conscious act. We can't take a training course to make it happen. It is a consequence of being in God's presence. So, when Jesus said, 'Let your light shine before others, that they may see your good deeds and glorify your Father in heaven' (Matthew 5:16, TNIV), he wasn't setting a difficult task. He knew that this was a lightweight burden—more like an invitation to spend time in his presence, becoming a friend of God, like Moses. As a result, the good deeds that we do will prompt people to praise God.

Other people's responses are not up to us. The Israelites wanted Moses' face covered up, and there are people today who want the light of Christ covered up, making it impossible for Christians to work openly in the name of Christ. But God promises that darkness will not overcome the light of God. There will always be some who see the quality of Christian life and work in families and communities and want to know more.

Meanwhile, the invitation is there for us to respond, to revel in God's love and delight in his presence. Over the next two weeks, as Chris Leonard helps us to look at the theme of light in the Bible, use this verse from Whittier's memorable hymn as a daily prayer.

Drop Thy still dews of quietness,
Till all our strivings cease;
Take from our souls the strain and stress,
And let our ordered lives confess
The beauty of Thy peace.
JOHN GREENLEAF WHITTIER (1807–92)

Reacting to the light

An angel of the Lord appeared to them, and the glory of the Lord shone around them, and they were terrified. But the angel said to them, 'Do not be afraid. I bring you good news of great joy that will be for all the people.'

Advent approaches, with its sense that light is dawning at the darkest time of year. Over the next two weeks we'll be asking, how do we react to that light? What is it, anyway, this light that sparkles or dazzles like powerful fibre-optic threads running throughout the Bible from Genesis to Revelation? What does it mean to our daily lives, to history, that God is light and that Jesus declared himself (and, more alarmingly, us his followers) to be the light of the world?

Let's start by asking how people reacted that first Christmas as Jesus' light came to earth. There was no great media event, no TV or Internet spectacular, no neon proclamations, just a poor, vulnerable baby. Maybe the only people outside so late at night were in the fields, attending the birth of lambs. The idea that the Lamb of God might be born would have been the last thing on their minds. Remember, no light pollution interrupted the blackness then. Imagine how the angelic host, in its most exuberant moment, dazzled and terrified the shepherds.

Few in the Old Testament who saw the *shekinah* glory of the Lord lived—but those shepherds, in the dark days of Roman occupation, did. Obedient to the strange message, they left precious sheep to seek a baby lying where cattle normally fed. Jesus would have seemed like any poor newborn but for their previous enlightenment. They reacted well, first by worshipping, like the angels, in spirit and in truth. Then they became the first human beings outside the holy family to tell others. I wonder how many believed them—and what happened to those who did, and did not? We don't know. We don't hear of the shepherds again. They were ordinary people, like you or me. Isn't that encouraging?

....

How do you react when God's light shines, dazzling or gentle, before you? In worship and wonder? In obedience? Do you find the courage and means to tell others, though they may find it incredible?

CL

Beginnings

The earth was formless and empty, darkness was over the surface of the deep… God said, 'Let there be light,' and there was light. God saw that the light was good, and he separated the light from the darkness. God called the light 'day', and the darkness he called 'night'.

These are strange words with which to describe the first 'day' of the earth. Even so long ago, surely the writer knew that light came from the sun, moon and stars—yet he recorded them as being created on day four. Those celestial lights were so vital for life that most people of the world in Old Testament times worshipped them in one way or another. Perhaps the writer of Genesis was playing down their importance?

If God is light, and if the celestial city doesn't need 'the light of a lamp or the light of the sun, for the Lord God will give them light' (Revelation 22:5), then maybe we shouldn't be surprised by light existing without its usual sources. It has been suggested that the pre-sun light in Genesis might have resembled something like the aurora borealis. I wouldn't know. But I have noticed how God separated light from darkness on both the first and the fourth 'days', and goes on separating them throughout the Bible, in one way or another.

When the earth was formless, empty and dark, 'the Spirit of God was hovering over the waters' (v. 2)—over the chaos, brooding things into being. And on the second day he separated something else—the waters from the dry land.

I'm so grateful that we don't live in a half-land half-sea swamp, though who knows what will result from global warming? I hope day stays separate from night: I should hate to live in a constant grey twilight. The way God has created it, each night provides an end to the day's troubles—a chance to sleep, to pray, to start again with a new dawn.

....

Picture how light transforms our surroundings—a rainbow against a dark sky, sunlight racing cloud shadows across the landscape, the eggshell blue of a winter sky reflected in water, snow light, fire light, star light… Imagine his light, and praise him!

CL

Ambiguities?

I will give you the treasures of darkness, riches stored in secret places, so that you may know that I am the Lord… who summons you by name… there is no other. I form the light and create darkness, I bring prosperity and create disaster; I, the Lord, do all these things.

We've just taken in how God separates light from darkness—yet here he's creating darkness, even giving people its treasures. He caused Cyrus, the pagan ruler of mighty Persia, to deliver his chosen people from the Babylonian exile to which he himself had sentenced them. That must have caused a few questions among the faithful!

Today, too, God is blamed for everything from floods and terrorism to a stubbed toe. 'If God is all light, all good, all powerful, then why do darkness, evil and suffering triumph so often?' Does the Lord, as the verses quoted above appear to suggest, cause them? No—read the whole chapter! Again and again it speaks of God's passion for righteousness, for saving the whole world, not just Israel. He even says, 'I have not spoken in secret, from somewhere in a land of darkness… I, the Lord, speak the truth; I declare what is right… for I am God, and there is no other… my mouth has uttered in all integrity a word that will not be revoked: before me every knee will bow; by me every tongue will swear' (vv. 19, 22–23). No ambiguity there!

Isaiah wrote of no moral mix-up. Having punished his erring people in order to draw them back to himself, God is restoring them with strength and love. Many religions of that time saw an equal battle between the gods of light and darkness, good and evil. But, no, there is one Lord of all. 'In the Lord alone are righteousness and strength' (v. 24, NIV). Even non-believers can be his servants. People were as adept in Isaiah's time as they are in ours at fudging morality and creating unrighteous ambiguity. Read Isaiah 5, especially verse 20: 'Woe to those… who put darkness for light and light for darkness.'

....

Think of occasions when you've heard God accused of causing harm, even evil. He doesn't need our defence, of course, but think how you might bring some truth, light, even good news to bear on the conversation, next time it happens.

CL

Knowing darkness, bringing light

'He reveals deep and hidden things; he knows what lies in darkness, and light dwells with him.'

If possible, read the first two chapters of Daniel. Exiled along with his people in Babylon, the young Daniel insists on praying to Yahweh and keeping the strict dietary rules of the Jewish religion, yet turns not a hair at learning alongside Babylon's astrologers. Isn't that surprising? Yet his ability to discern good from evil isn't impaired. Bravely, he tells autocratic King Nebuchadnezzar, 'No wise man, enchanter, magician or diviner can explain to the king the mystery he has asked about, but there is a God in heaven who reveals mysteries' (vv. 27–28). Daniel then proceeds to tell the king what none of his wise men or astrologers could—first recounting the king's dream, then interpreting it.

I shy away from contact with anything occult or any kind of darkness—but thank God he knows what lies there! Satan, of course, 'masquerades as an angel of light' in a fallen world (2 Corinthians 11:14). No wonder we mere mortals struggle with moral ambiguities. If God requires us, like Daniel, to look into darkness, we must take great care. Even saints can be corrupted and false apostles do exist.

On the other hand, few people are so evil that there is no good in them. Few circumstances are so dark that we can't see God shining his light there, bringing good. Sometimes we are called to be his agents. It's painful and risky, but our God of light and holiness has shown us the way: 'Darkness came over the whole land until three in the afternoon, for the sun stopped shining… Jesus called out with a loud voice, "Father, into your hands I commit my spirit." When he had said this, he breathed his last. The centurion, seeing what had happened, praised God and said, "Surely this was a righteous man"' (Luke 23:44–47).

....

Meditate on how that pagan centurion at the crucifixion was one of the first to see God's extraordinary separation of light and darkness, which brought about your salvation and, perhaps, his own.

CL

In your light we see light

Transgression speaks to the wicked deep in their hearts; there is no fear of God before their eyes... With you is the fountain of life; in your light we see light.

Sometimes a phrase from the Bible leaps out and hits us between the eyes. 'In your light we see light' did that for me, many years ago. I could sense its importance but what did it mean, exactly? Our light comes from sun, moon, electricity: how do we see that light, see our world, in God's light? At the time I was studying English and theology at university. I'd met some dynamic Christians; the Bible was coming alive to me as something to live by; my faith and my love for Jesus were growing. How could my theology lectures, based on that same Bible, be so utterly boring, irrelevant and even plain wrong? (Today's study of theology, thankfully, has improved out of all recognition.)

Some editions of the NRSV subtitle Psalm 36 'Human wickedness and divine goodness'—light and darkness in the moral sense. I don't believe that my theology lecturers were morally wicked and most had the title 'Revd', so I assume they had had a real faith at some point. But perhaps there was no real 'fear of God before their eyes', as the psalm says. Was their dominant fear a fear of academia, which, in the 1970s, tended to put beyond the pale anyone who believed in the supernatural? Maybe academic standards were the light in which they saw light.

By what light do we see light? Seeing the dawn, moonlight or sun sparkling on water, seeing light filtered through fresh green or fiery autumn leaves, seeing any beauty in God's creation, including the beauty within the Bible and in people, in goodness and the creative arts—don't our hearts lift? Don't we respond to him in praise and thankfulness, because we know him, we know the one who dreamt all this up? In his light we see light—and know that it is very good.

....

As the psalm suggests, in his light we see darkness too. The darkness may sadden him but it's not dark to him (Psalm 139:11–12).

CL

Light for guidance

Let those who walk in the dark, who have no light, trust in the name of the Lord and rely on their God. But now, all you who light fires and provide yourselves with flaming torches, go, walk in the light of your fires and of the torches you have set ablaze.

Guidance… so often we feel we're walking in the dark. Why can't God just write something in the sky? The prophet has been asking, 'Who among you fears the Lord and obeys the word of his servant?' (50:10). Before that, one of Isaiah's 'servant songs' prophesies clearly about Jesus, who 'set my face like flint' and 'offered my back to those who beat me' (vv. 6, 7). If we walk in Jesus' light, we'll have no easy life, but perhaps guidance isn't meant to be easy. We will learn to listen to the Lord and learn 'the word that sustains the weary' (v. 4). Walking in the dark teaches us to listen, in humility. People deprived of sight pay more attention to sound and follow their guide closely, trusting absolutely, even when the road leads them through some very difficult places.

By contrast, society teaches us to be self-reliant. Isaiah's prophecy gives hefty judgment against those who 'light their own torches', perhaps seeking guidance from elsewhere—through occult means or simply choosing the most profitable or easy path with no reference to God. We're told to 'look to… the quarry from which you were hewn; look to Abraham, your father' (51:1–2). God blessed and guided him, yet you could say that Abraham 'lit his own torch', trying to fulfil God's promise of an heir prematurely by sleeping with his servant-girl. They produced Ishmael, whose descendants brought continuing trouble. When we go our own way, the consequences can be heavy. Yet, as the prophecy emphasizes, God's salvation never fails.

When it comes to guidance, things seem clear… looking back. At the time, we have to trust that God will lead us through, even though we don't always recognize him doing so until afterwards.

....

Can you see the way ahead—one step at a time? Psalm 119:105 says that his word is 'a lamp to my feet', but we can't always see that light shining ahead. Thank God that he can, and that he knows what he is doing.

CL

Only the broken let in the light

You, Lord, are my lamp; the Lord turns my darkness into light. With your help I can advance against a troop; with my God I can scale a wall.

David sang the words of this song when the Lord delivered him from the hand of all his enemies, and Saul. Broken, nearly killed, betrayed, bereaved, rescued by God—David did a few wicked and many great things. As the Lord turned his darkness into light, he wrote songs. This one, recorded at the end of his life, seems definitive.

At a secular gig, I puzzled over how the songs of Duke Special from Belfast could be full of pain, yet so uplifting. Then he deviated from the words and music on his album to repeat something like, 'Only the broken let in the light.' Moved, I wondered where I had heard that before. In the Bible? No, though I remembered a Christian mime artist using a large broken jar to illustrate that we are all broken: we have to be in order for God to fill us. As 2 Corinthians 4:7 and 10 say, 'We have this treasure in jars of clay to show that this all-surpassing power is from God and not from us… We always carry around in our body the death of Jesus, so that the life of Jesus may also be revealed.'

Later I found the words, in a National Trust magazine article about their butterfly expert, Matthew Oates. Only happy when wild butterflies are happy, this true eccentric has done much good for wildlife. His motto? 'Blessed are the cracked, for they let in the light.' An Internet search revealed 'It's the ones who've cracked that the light shines through'—a 2003 album by Jeffrey Lewis. I could imagine Jesus saying those words.

Someone phoned the other day. She had been bereaved within the past three months. 'It's amazing how I've been able to get alongside others, relate to them in a far deeper way, help them, even. I hadn't expected that, not amidst my own emotional turmoil,' she told me.

....

Read Micah 7:1–9 for another example of a broken man trusting that God 'will bring me out into the light'. Don't hide, or fear, your own broken places. Let his light shine through them.

CL

Has our light come?

Arise, shine; for your light has come, and the glory of the Lord has risen upon you. For darkness shall cover the earth, and thick darkness the peoples; but the Lord will arise upon you, and his glory will appear over you.

What a wonderful passage for Advent Sunday. But the question is, does it—does light shine, does holy glory rest on God's people? Was that true in Isaiah's day? The nation's return from exile, though miraculous, wasn't that bright and glorious. They struggled to rebuild their lives and walls, their worship and nation. Starting with good intentions, soon they slipped into the same bad ways again. What about now, long after Jesus came to proclaim good news and 'the year of the Lord's favour'? There's still darkness within the church, and news across the world seems ever blacker—or is that down to the media's reporting?

On a more trivial note, I confess that this is my least favourite time of year. As days grow darker, the busyness and hype of Christmas leave me weary and cynical. Soon there will be plenty of lights in the darkness, flashing annoyingly in the shape of vast plastic snowmen or luring us to hysterical mass worship of materialism in shopping malls. Sons may 'come from afar' to stay with us, alongside assorted great-aunts. The hearts of those of us who entertain them are unlikely to 'thrill and rejoice' at the prospect, because 'peace' may not arrive to be the overseer. Instead, the Herculean task of keeping several generations happy within a confined space falls to us women.

Jesus' coming did bring light, of course: he liberated captives, bound up the broken-hearted, comforted the mourners and all the rest of it. But this world is still full of darkness, conflict, cruelty, selfishness—and my heart is, too. His light can shine in and through us only as we look to him. May we let him shine for us, in us and through us, until that day when his light has come fully and darkness is no more.

....

I'm so grateful that the Bible is no spin-doctor. It acknowledges that shining light into the darkness costs, but it costs the Lord even more than it costs us.

CL

Life and light—on the winning side

What has come into being in him was life, and the life was the light of all people. The light shines in the darkness, and the darkness did not overcome it.

Last week we looked at Genesis and now we see that before the beginning of light there was the Word: the preincarnate Jesus took part in the very creation of light for our world. Do read all of today's extraordinarily potent verses if you can.

I'm interested in life being equated with light. Very little life exists without light in the natural world—down caves, in mines or the deepest oceans, for example. Nearly everything on our planet owes its existence to the sun's energy—and all to the Son's.

I'm even more interested in the words 'the darkness did not overcome it'—or, in the NIV, 'the darkness has not understood it'. Darkness does not understand light. Creatures living in caves are dazzled by it and often lose their ability to see it altogether. If you're familiar with *The Lord of the Rings*, think how Gollum illustrates the moral consequences of living in darkness. Or think of someone who simply can't understand why a person would take a morally righteous decision if it brought no benefit to him- or herself. But the Greek word doesn't simply mean understanding or even enlightenment. As in the NRSV, it encompasses an element of conflict: the darkness cannot 'overcome' the light. One tiny candle can chase away darkness but darkness can never extinguish a candle.

I find it hard to see myself with a kind of lightsabre, slicing into the world's darkness on Christ's behalf, and I find God's glorious holiness so awesome and dazzling that I can't possibly understand it. But even when we find ourselves in dark places, don't we see little candles of light? And don't they begin to add up, one by one, so that we begin to be ready to glimpse his glory again?

....

Bearing enlightenment and conflict in mind, read Matthew 16:15–19, not forgetting that all potential overcoming here is done not by the gates but by the church—you and me, battering them down.

CL

The Lord's light

*From… his waist up he looked like glowing metal, as if full of fire…
and brilliant light surrounded him. Like the appearance of a rainbow
in the clouds on a rainy day, so was the radiance around him… the
glory of the Lord. When I saw it, I fell face down.*

'God is light; in him there is no darkness at all,' says 1 John 1:5. Some
of the most awesome pictures of God in the whole Bible show him,
and show the risen, glorified Jesus, as holy (and wholly) dazzling light.
Today's passage in Revelation is very similar to that in Ezekiel, right
down to the human response. And, of course, when Jesus was transfigured in front of his three closest friends, 'His face shone like the sun,
and his clothes became as white as the light' (Matthew 17:2).

This blinding, holy, glorious light is awesome—it scares me, as well
it might. 1 Timothy 6:16 speaks of God as the one 'who alone is immortal and who lives in unapproachable light'. He seems so remote,
and yet Psalm 44:3 says that Israel won the promised land not through
their own strength but by 'your right hand, your arm, and the light of
your face, for you loved them'. Light allied to love is something else!

A friend of mine has just returned from Antony Gormley's art instal-
lation, 'Blind Light', at the Hayward Gallery in London. Inside a cloud-
filled glass room, literally all you can see is light. At first my friend was
apprehensive. Would she be able to breathe in there or find her way
out again? Wouldn't people bump into one another? Cautiously she felt
her way along the glass wall. She could hear parents' worried calls:
'Where are you, Anna? Joe, come back!' Then she realized that children
were running, joyously, without fear. 'Is this heaven?' she heard one
ask. Soon adults, too, were likening the experience to paradise. Awed,
out of control and at first afraid, they were none the less safe. They too
began to move freely, to enjoy themselves. Unless we become like little children, maybe we can't enter into God's light, either!

....

*Talk to God about approaching the light of his holiness boldly, as a
child might—and read Hebrews 12:18–24 to help you.*

CL

105

Children of light

You were once darkness, but now you are light in the Lord. Live as children of light (for the fruit of the light consists in all goodness, righteousness and truth) and find out what pleases the Lord… Everything exposed by the light becomes visible.

Many biblical references to light concern morality—usually, as here, in a very positive form. This is less about 'thou shalt not' than the far more difficult 'find out what pleases the Lord', which calls us to live in a way that is good, righteous and true. Paul assures us that the love of Christ motivates and the Holy Spirit helps us.

An article in an American daily newspaper struck me recently. The writer, Tom Krattenmaker, while sympathetic to Christianity, questioned how extremes of violence, poverty and riches can prevail in a nation where the majority read the Bible, pray, attend church, give generously to charity and help their neighbours. Most American Christians live broadly 'good, righteous and true' lives, as do you and I. That's what made me giggle during a group Bible study on the story of Ahab, Jezebel and Naboth's vineyard in 1 Kings 21. We were asked, 'How does your behaviour reflect Ahab's?' 'When has anyone in this room caused anyone to be murdered or stolen someone's land?' I chortled. Then I saw how Ahab, failing to get his own way, sank into a real sulk. The rest of his sorry tale followed from that attitude. Hmm. I have been known to sulk, to be selfish, even to abuse the little power I have… Exposed again, by the Bible!

Everything exposed to light becomes visible. Living in the light, we're meant to reflect it into dark places. Maybe that's what most Western Christians don't do effectively. If we truly seek to live in the light of what pleases God, then we need to pay more attention to his constant heart-cry for the poor and marginalized. Perhaps the niceties of church services or even issues of sexuality hijack too much attention!

....

What does it mean to you, in practical terms, to be a child of the light?

CL

What light shines from you?

'The eye is the lamp of the body. If your eyes are healthy, your whole body will be full of light. But if your eyes are unhealthy, your whole body will be full of darkness. If then the light within you is darkness, how great is that darkness!'

What light is shining from you and me right now? Has it become muddied? In this passage, Jesus suggests various ways in which that might happen, including hypocrisy, worry, loving material things more than God, and judging others.

U2's blistering song 'Crumbs from your table' draws on an image that Jesus might have used, had people at the time understood the workings of our universe. The biggest, shiniest star in the universe may eventually collapse in on itself, sucking the life out of everything as it becomes the most powerful 'black hole'. The song says that if Jesus' followers—the Church—turn bad, that is what happens. When good has been corrupted totally, so that it does the opposite of what it was created for, then 'how great is that darkness!' Think Inquisition; think Crusades and modern sectarian violence; think rich Christians indifferent to those dying of poverty.

Although light may escape through the impurity of our wrong attitudes, however, most of us aren't 'black holes'. Think of all the ways, every day, in which the Lord does make his people shine.

U2's sometime producer, Brian Eno, created '77 Million Paintings'. In fact, he made far fewer but projected them randomly so that various ones interwove, slowly, each changing colour and size. As one faded, another grew. Eno changed light as subtly as a synthesizer can change sound, giving a fascinating, restful experience, with beautiful if random combinations. Dream about how, together, we can shine, each in different ways with different colours, shapes, lines and patterns—some prominent now, others later.

....

If you allow the Lord to be the 'projectionist', how will you shine this Christmas-time, and how might your shining blend with that of others? Ask him!

CL

Loving light

Blessed are those who have learned to acclaim you, who walk in the light of your presence, Lord. They rejoice in your name all day long; they exult in your righteousness. For you are their glory and strength, and by your favour you exalt our horn.

'Press 14,' she'd said. I did, several times, but remained standing in the rain in front of an obstinately closed door, peering at instructions printed below a number pad. In dim light, these days, I need glasses for reading, but they weren't with me. Eventually someone arrived and told me to press '#' first. 'Open sesame!'

The older I become, the more I love light. As well as helping me to see and understand things, it gives me energy. Staying at home in the cosy glow of a winter's evening is all very well but, if I'm not exposed to enough light, I tend towards gloom. Seasonal Affective Disorder, they call it. Mine would be a mild form but, when a little 'SAD' in the dark days of winter, I'm especially grateful for the light of the Lord's presence. Of course, walking in his light is good any time of year. Truth and understanding are so much better than lies and prejudice.

The Light of the world is so inclusive. No one has to remain in confusion on the doorstep. Jesus said, 'I have come into the world as a light, so that no one who believes in me should stay in darkness' (John 12:46). You will need to read the rest of John 12:30–50 to see how he was 'lifted up': it's an extraordinary picture of Jesus, dazzling in his agony on the cross against the backdrop of all the darkness that evil could throw at him. However near to or far from him we are at the moment, we can allow ourselves to be drawn towards that light of truth, salvation and love. Or we can turn away and try to hide in darkness, where we'll bump painfully into people and things, unable to see a way out, damaging ourselves and others.

....

Read John 3:1–21. The image of seeing and being drawn towards the light, away from the darkness, is so much more helpful, I find, than that of being 'born again', especially when talking with those who don't yet know Jesus.

CL

You are the light of the world

'You are the light of the world. A city built on a hill cannot be hidden. No one after lighting a lamp puts it under the bushel basket, but on the lampstand, and it gives light to all in the house... Let your light shine before others, that they may see your good works and give glory to your Father in heaven.'

In his most famous sermon, Jesus, born to be the Light of the world, tells his ragtag collection of followers that they are the light of the world! That must have come as quite a shock, although from Jesus' point of view it's logical. Consider John 8:12: 'When Jesus spoke again to the people, he said, "I am the light of the world. Whoever follows me will never walk in darkness, but will have the light of life"' (TNIV).

The context of Matthew 5 is the new covenant, which sets out Jesus' moral standards for those who would relate to him. They are far more stringent than those in the Commandments given through Moses. Jesus' hearers must have been reeling with shock after that sermon. He starts with the apparently upside-down world of the Beatitudes, where the poor and meek and persecuted are 'happy'. To us the words sound familiar but a closer examination makes me most uncomfortable. How can I possess the righteousness of Christ or fulfil his role in being the light of the world? Do people see my good deeds and glorify God for them? Very, very occasionally, perhaps. But then he is, in the words of Wesley's great carol, the 'Sun of righteousness'.

Philippians 2:14–15 compares us to stars, which are faint from the perspective of people on earth, so they can only be seen at night: 'Do all things without murmuring and arguing, so that you may be blameless and innocent, children of God without blemish in the midst of a crooked and perverse generation, in which you shine like stars in the world' (NRSV). None of us can hope to be the light of the world all by ourselves but, together, like the Milky Way, we do shine.

....

Take stock of what and who you really love. When our passions are aligned with the Lord's, don't we each burn brighter, bringing more warmth and light and love to those around?

CL

As Chris Leonard says in her notes for 30 November, there is still much darkness in the world, despite the fact that Jesus has come as its Light.

In prayer, though, we can play a part in bringing his light to bear on the dark situations of life—light that the darkness can neither understand nor overcome.

Here are some lines of prayer that you could use to ask Jesus to illuminate the lives of people you know, or people in the news today. (There is nothing to stop you, of course, from praying in your own words or for different circumstances of darkness that are not covered below.)

Light of the world,

For _____ , who cannot see a way through the financial problems that threaten to overwhelm them, let there be light.

For _____ , struggling with relationship difficulties that seem insoluble, let there be light.

For _____ , worn down by depression, grief or fear, let there be light.

For _____ , unable to forgive the terrible hurt inflicted on them in years gone by, let there be light.

For _____ , trapped in a life of crime or abuse, let there be light.

For _____ , unable to break free from addiction, let there be light.

For _____ , who after all these years still cannot accept salvation through faith in you, let there be light.

Lord Jesus, take these broken people into your care and let your light in through the cracks. Bring them into a full knowledge of your glory, for the sake of your kingdom. Amen

Have you ever visited an embassy? Perhaps you've needed to get a visa to travel overseas or maybe you've been stranded abroad and have visited the embassy to get help. An embassy is a tiny outpost of a country: when I went to the Ugandan Embassy recently, the waiting-room television was showing Ugandan programmes and the décor was Ugandan, as were the staff. It gave me a glimpse of the country itself.

Have you ever thought of your home as an embassy—an embassy of heaven? This is another aspect of letting our light shine before other people. If our homes are embassies of heaven, they are places where our neighbours, relatives, friends and workmates can have a taste of heaven, somewhere they can meet with Jesus and experience what it's like to be part of his kingdom. To become an embassy of heaven, we need to respond with a resounding 'Yes!' to Paul's command, 'Practise hospitality' (Romans 12:13, TNIV). Over the next two weeks, Sylvia Mandeville, who is new to the *Day by Day with God* team of contributors, takes up the topic of hospitality. She says:

These 14 readings can only touch on the subject, but I hope they give us a glimpse of its profound roots. Hospitality is God's idea—it is at the very heart of his nature. And, as with any aspect of God's character, it takes a lifetime to plumb the depths of its meaning and to make God's upside-down viewpoint our own.

In the West we read about corporate hospitality where firms book expensive suites to entertain clients at special events. The aim is to impress the guests, to lure them to do business. Nothing could be further from God's ideas on hospitality. He is interested in the vulnerable, the poor, the needy. He does not want to impress. He wants to welcome and restore.

But there is also a mystery—the mystery of the incarnation. Christ, the Son of God, calls us to himself with outstretched arms from the cross so that we can receive the hospitality of forgiveness from him. He also passionately wants to be our guest and to live within us.

As we consider the ministry of hospitality, ask God to help you become more aware of his welcome for you and, through you, to pass it on to the vulnerable, poor and needy.

An offer too good to refuse

Come, all you who are thirsty, come to the waters; and you who have no money, come, buy and eat! Come, buy wine and milk without money and without cost. Why spend money on what is not bread, and your labour on what does not satisfy?

It was a sunny day and, as a treat, our teacher had taken us outside to sit on the grass for our RE lesson. She opened her Bible and read the words above: 'Come, all you who are thirsty, come to the waters' (v. 1). A great yearning rose in me. I did not understand the full meaning of those words, but the invitation for the thirsty to 'come' drew me. The experience stayed deep within my inner life. Years later, when new life with Jesus was a reality to me and I read similar words spoken by Christ —'those who drink the water I give them will never thirst' (John 4:14)— I recognized the nature of the invitation that I had sensed so long ago. Now I realize that this wonderful offer of refreshment is a reflection of God's hospitality, which he is daily offering to each one of us.

In fact, God is into hospitality in a big way—ever since he created the beautiful garden of Eden and gave it to Adam and Eve for their delight. Hospitality is a running theme throughout the Bible. It expresses the very nature of God. As his children, we allow his Spirit to make us more like him and so we should make ourselves available for him to develop this ministry in us. Don't be surprised if he grabs the most unexpected people for you to entertain.

Isaiah 55 is an invitation to share in all the riches God offers us in the new order that he is bringing in. It is an invitation to rich and poor alike, and to people of all nations. This is an offer not confined to the Jewish people beloved of God. Although written long before Christ was born, it gives a glimpse of God's broader plan and vision for all humankind. This caring for the poor and needy was a deep concern of Christ. As we obey him, it should be our concern, too.

....

If you yourself have received God's hospitality, be ready to offer hospitality. It may mean sharing a sandwich at work, treating a Big Issue seller to a cup of tea or sharing how Christ has given you refreshment with someone you meet. Let God teach you!

SM

Lavish extravagance

On this mountain the Lord Almighty will prepare a feast of rich food for all peoples, a banquet of aged wine—the best of meats and the finest of wines.

I remember the joy I felt when preparing our daughter's wedding. Years before, Tim and I had had an extremely modest wedding, with the reception held in a friend's house. I think I had less than ten pounds in the bank at the time. But, for our daughter, I wanted to lavish all we had on her—nothing but the best—and I have never regretted that splash of extravagance.

Yesterday's reading showed God's generous hospitality towards us when he offers us the essentials: a spring of water welling up for eternal life. Today we read about an extravagant banquet to which all are invited, to enjoy choice food and plenty to drink. It's a celebration of generosity and variety, of unrestrained rejoicing, and nothing will be spared to make the occasion spectacular—when death will be swallowed up in victory (vv. 6–9). Yes, this is our God. This is his nature—to offer us hospitality with no begrudging, lavishly laying it out before us.

The film *Babette's Feast* tells the story of a refugee, Babette, who stays with two very austere Christian sisters. They keep every economy, live very frugally and penny-pinch on everything. Their lives are colourless and dreary. Then Babette hears that she has come into a modest inheritance. What should she do with it? She asks if she can cook the two sisters a meal. For days she plans and prepares, shops and cooks. When the sisters are invited to the table, it is piled high with delights—colourful fruits, exquisite pies and cakes. There are delicious smells and tastes they never knew existed. What a wonderful feast! And Babette has blown all her money on it. She knows that there is a time to celebrate and a time to be lavish as well as a time to economize.

....

Do you allow enough space in your life for celebration? Smelling a rose, absorbing a sunset or hugging a child all count—and they are not extravagant!

SM

What are the implications for me?

'For I was hungry and you gave me something to eat, I was thirsty and you gave me something to drink, I was a stranger and you invited me in, I needed clothes and you clothed me.'

Martha and Mary in Bethany were able to invite Jesus into their home, knowing who he was (Luke 10:38–42). How I would love to have been there, to offer rest and refreshment to Jesus in reality. But this parable makes an astonishing claim: I can still have Christ as a guest in my own home. So far, we have looked at two aspects of God's hospitality in all its generosity and splendour. In this parable, Jesus gets down to the nitty-gritty of daily hospitality among the poor and needy. He speaks directly to us, and it makes for rather uncomfortable reading. What do you think of this astonishing statement? 'The King will reply, "Truly I tell you, whatever you did for one of the least of these brothers and sisters of mine, you did for me"' (v. 40).

Does this mean that when we give money to dig a well in a village in Africa, we're really giving Christ the means to have a drink? When we give clothes to a charity appeal for earthquake victims, are we clothing Christ? It's a tough thought for us to get our heads around. The converse is equally disturbing: if we ignore people in need, then we are ignoring Christ himself. If we belong to Christ, if we allow his nature to take root in us and transform us, then being hospitable in a variety of ways is an inescapable part of that process. We are not free to say, 'I keep myself to myself' or 'We don't entertain; only family, that's what counts.' We are missing opportunities to receive Jesus himself as our guest.

In today's mobile world, where people move frequently to work in different parts of the country, there is a great need for hospitality. Many churches now make sure refreshments are offered at the end of services, to welcome newcomers especially. That is good, but one step better is to invite the newcomer home for a meal.

....

Do you feel threatened by the idea that Christ will involve you in hospitality of some kind? Keeping in mind verse 40 from today's reading, read Hebrews 13:2 and discover who else might be drinking out of one of your mugs.

SM

God's planning ahead

'In my Father's house are many rooms; if it were not so, I would have told you. I am going there to prepare a place for you.'

Pause and imagine for a moment the setting of this reading. The disciples have just shared the last supper with Jesus. Imagine the confused panic that the disciples were feeling. Jesus has said that one of them will betray him and that Peter will deny him. The hardest shock of all was his warning to them that he would be going away (vv. 1–4). Knowing and living alongside Jesus had turned their world upside down. How could they survive? What would life be like without him?

Into this bewilderment Jesus gives them a wonderful promise. 'In my Father's house are many rooms... I am going there to prepare a place for you' (v. 2).

On a long and tiring journey, how nice it is to think about the arrival: the welcome, the cup of tea and bed. Today's reading gives us a hint of how we should feel about our long and often wearying Christian journey. We should think of the welcome and the room that God has ready for us. Jesus our Lord is going ahead to prepare a place and a welcome for us. Can we really take that in?

But there is more! What else has he planned for us? It is always special to know that a welcome is assured when we go anywhere, but to be met and taken there completes the joy (v. 3).

Once, we came back late at night from a long trip to Central Asia. We had left behind hot sunshine, but we knew snow was on the ground in Manchester. To our delight, some friends had come to meet us. Not only was their car ready and waiting to take us home, but it was warm and on the back seat were blankets and a hot water bottle. What a welcome! What forward planning!

Of course we have to live here in this world, but what a joyous perspective to think that one day we shall be taken to heavenly mansions.

....

Could the balance of my life be shifted slightly so that I have a more heavenly perspective? Does anyone else know where I am heading and who my host is?

SM

On the lookout

'Let's make a small room on the roof and put in it a bed and a table, a chair and a lamp for him. Then he can stay there whenever he comes to us.'

Yesterday we read about God's wonderful forward planning for being hospitable towards us. Today's reading takes us to the ninth century BC in Israel, where a woman grasps the same idea. She shows three key essentials in the ministry of hospitality. First, she noticed who was passing by and responded. Elisha's travels through her area caught her attention. Second, she was sensitive to his needs: he would be tired and hungry from walking on hot, dusty roads. Third, she was practical in her response: 'Let's make a small room…' she suggested to her husband, and together they put the plan into action.

We have some friends who did exactly the same as the Shunammite woman, except that they made a loft conversion in the roof rather than a room on the roof! They felt the Lord urging them to make use of the space and, although they did not have enough money for the whole project, they took a step of faith. They booked a builder and a date for the work to begin. Just in time, the husband was given an unexpected pay rise and they were able to pay the bills. As they put in the finishing touches, their pastor rang with an urgent request. 'There is a young man coming to work locally from the country. He is desperate for accommodation with a Christian family. Can you help?' They were so glad they had been obedient and stepped out in faith.

Elisha must have been delighted when he was shown his special room and he did not take it for granted (v. 13). The Shunammite's modest answer to him, when he offered to speak in high places on her behalf, indicates her godly humility. But Elisha's servant had empathy for her real need: she had no son. Elisha promised her that by the same time the following year, she should have a child, and so it was.

....

Have you noticed anyone who needs hospitality? What are his or her particular needs? Is there any way you could supply some or all of them?

SM

Welcome! Welcome!

Abraham looked up and saw three men standing nearby. When he saw them, he hurried from the entrance of his tent to meet them and bowed low to the ground... 'Let a little water be brought, and then you may all wash your feet and rest under this tree.'

Although Abraham does not use the word 'welcome', his every gesture and word expresses it. As soon as he saw the men, he hurried out to meet them—even though he himself was old and resting in the heat of the day. What essentials in a hot and dusty country does he immediately offer (vv. 4–5)? Can you notice the same three essential characteristics of hospitality observed in yesterday's reading? Observation, sensitivity and practicality—all vital, and Abraham showed them all.

There are so many people in this world who are desperate for a welcome. A Somali student I know went with his wife to a UK university. He was involved all day with lectures, library work and essays. His wife sat alone in her flat and was too timid to go out. No one made any contact with her. She might as well have been invisible. No one offered her a warm gesture. After several terms of this unhappy isolation, she left her husband and got a divorce. What sad and unnecessary suffering! Were there no Christians around to invite her for coffee? Just one Christian woman, aware and sensitive to her needs, could have transformed that poor wife's misery.

Abraham's hospitality cost him, his wife and servants time, energy and provisions. Any hospitality we offer will also cost the same, but in welcoming people into our homes, our journeys and our churches, we are given opportunities to reflect God's very nature.

Little did Abraham know, when he ran out to meet his guests, what life-changing events were about to occur (v. 10). Of course we should not offer hospitality with an eye to rewards, but God sometimes surprises us with some very unexpected ones.

....

If you find it hard to have unexpected changes to your routine or interruptions to your day, say this quick prayer before you answer the door or the phone: 'Lord, help me to welcome with love and practical help whoever is phoning or standing on the doorstep.'

SM

117

Welcome back!

'But while he was still a long way off, his father saw him and was filled with compassion for him; he ran to his son, threw his arms round him and kissed him.'

Many artists and sculptors through the centuries have tried to capture this dramatic scene: the thud of impact as father and son are reunited, the tears, the joy, the relief, the fulfilment of dreams. It is the happy ending we all long for in every unhappy story.

This is the third parable that Jesus tells on the same theme, and Luke sets them alongside each other in the same chapter. The prodigal son, the lost sheep (vv. 1–7) and the lost coin (vv. 8–10) all have the same theme: something lost and something found.

Today's reading tells the lost-and-found story in the most detail. It is dealing with complex human relationships and the depth of feeling between a father and son. After the previous two parables, Jesus explains them. As the shepherd and the woman rejoice at finding the sheep and the coin, Jesus says, 'I tell you, there is rejoicing in the presence of the angels of God over one sinner who repents' (v. 10). I wonder why Christ does not make any comment about his third parable. Perhaps, as he told this moving story, he could sense that his audience had grasped its deepest meaning. The father runs to the son. There are no retributions, just love and forgiveness and rejoicing.

Out of interest, whereabouts are you standing as you read? Do you identify with the repentant son weeping at his father's feet or are you the father whose heart has been torn with pain and is now daring to believe that his son is truly home again?

The story does not end with the ecstatic welcome, the tears and the hugs. The father wants to celebrate: 'Quick, bring the best robe and put it on him,' he orders a servant. What else does he prepare for his son? (v. 23).

Dramatic scenes in family life, especially when rifts need to be healed, are often best nurtured with a meal. I often feel this sense of welcome back when I take Communion. Christ himself hands me the bread and the wine and we are at peace together.

SM

Hospitality in the workplace

'Even if she gathers among the sheaves, don't embarrass her. Rather, pull out some stalks for her from the bundles and leave them for her to pick up, and don't rebuke her.'

Hospitality is not always about food, though food is a very important part of it. In this restful pastoral story, another aspect is shown—how to be hospitable at work. There is such an urgent need for this today in factory, office, school, hospital, shop or farm, wherever work is done.

Ruth is a foreigner and here she is picking up barley stalks in Boaz' field. This work was always done by the poorest widows and the needy. How easily the gleaners could have driven this foreign woman away. After all, she is taking barley that they could have for themselves. The boss, Boaz, fortunately has more godly values. How observant and sensitive Boaz is, and what practical suggestions he makes. Read Leviticus 23:22: do you think this verse may have taught Boaz how to treat the poor and alien?

In today's workplace, there are many people like Ruth—poor, hard-working, needy foreigners doing humble tasks. What is your attitude to them—or do you not even notice them? Is there any way you can learn from Boaz to make such people feel safe and accepted at work? You may have to go against the attitudes and remarks of your fellow workers to achieve this. Find the verses that reveal Boaz' care.

- Permission to work: vv. _____
- Provision of refreshment: v. _____
- Welcome into the 'staff canteen': v. _____

Everyone new to a work situation needs to be made welcome—not only the lowly paid but even the boss or director or a new pastor or vicar. Cakes, cards and flowers are the traditional means of welcome, but can you be creative and think of other ways?

....

Is there any newcomer in your life? In the choir, on a church committee, at work or in your neighbourhood? Pause and listen to how God would like you to reach out in friendship to that person.

SM

Risky hospitality

So the king of Jericho sent this message to Rahab: 'Bring out the men who came to you and entered your house, because they have come to spy out the whole land.' But the woman had taken the two men and hidden them.

Hospitality is not always about jolly welcomes, good food and comfy beds. There can be a serious and sometimes risky side to having someone to stay. Rahab certainly found that, and so have countless other people through the ages. Corrie ten Boom, the Dutch watchmaker's daughter, and her sister hid Jewish families in their home during World War II. French Resistance workers hid British airmen and other secret agents at great risk to themselves. Why were they doing it? I have often pondered on their courage.

It must be, I think, a question of allegiance. Rahab had heard about God's power working on behalf of the Israelites (vv. 10–11). She now wanted to change her allegiance from the local gods of Jericho to the mighty God of heaven. She was prepared to hide the spies if they in turn promised to spare her family when the Israelites attacked. It was a big risk. The king of Jericho's soldiers could well have searched her house and found the barely concealed men, but the greater good and a glimpse of faith gave Rahab courage.

Similar situations may not happen to us in peace time but, in other parts of the world, Christians fleeing from persecution may well seek refuge with other believers. If you have young children, do you put them at risk to shelter others? We have offered shelter to a woman whose boyfriend is abusive and violent. If she accepts, how do we answer the door if the boyfriend and comes shouting and swearing to the house? Some people give accommodation to failed asylum seekers who otherwise would be destitute and homeless. How should they respond to the knock on the door? These are difficult questions to come to terms with.

....

Families in countries where Christians are persecuted often have to flee their area and go into hiding. Christians, who may not even know them, risk much by receiving them into their homes. Prayer support for them is vital.

SM

Guest or host? A mystery

Here I am! I stand at the door and knock. If anyone hears my voice and opens the door, I will come in and eat with them and they with me.

This powerful and famous verse is often used as the text for a gospel message, but it was actually written to the Christians in Laodicea, calling them to repent (v. 19). We are so familiar with the words, but have you ever thought what they reveal about hospitality? Outside, Christ himself stands as a would-be guest. He is hoping we will open the door and allow him to come in. Then the surprise! Jesus does not say that he will come in and be waited on by us. No, Jesus sets the agenda: 'If anyone… opens the door, I will come in and eat with them and they with me.' With that one sentence, the roles are reversed. We invite Christ in as a guest, but as he sits at the table, he becomes the host: we are eating with him.

In *Prayer for All Times* (Fount), Pierre Charles explores this idea. He describes Jesus sitting at our table, sharing our evening meal. The encounter continues into the gentle calm and silence of the night, where confidences are exchanged. We need to meet Christ like this, in repose, so that he can give us his peace and we can allow time for mysteries to be revealed. The disciples on the road to Emmaus had such an experience. Do read Luke 24:13–32 again and enjoy the way Christ, the invited guest, becomes the host and reveals himself to them.

The most precious example of this is when we receive Holy Communion or share in the breaking of bread. As we receive the bread and wine, we receive Christ himself into our life. We can leave it at that or we can welcome him and permit him to become our host and perhaps even rearrange the furniture.

Come risen Lord, and deign to be our guest; Nay, let us be thy guests, the feast is thine; Thyself at thine own board made manifest, In thine own sacrament of bread and wine.
GEORGE WALLACE BRIGGS (1875–1959)

SM

Hospitality at the cutting edge

When foreigners reside among you in your land, do not ill-treat them. The foreigners residing among you must be treated as your native-born. Love him as yourself, for you were foreigners in Egypt.

These verses from Leviticus are uncomfortable, as are the verses in Luke. They strike at the root of our attitudes, our hearts, even our politics. They present us with a challenge wherever we live. We no longer have to travel abroad to meet other nationalities. The world's peoples have come to us and we must welcome them and love them.

Our home town is a dispersal town for asylum seekers. Suddenly it has changed from a homely market town to a place bustling with new faces, new ways of dressing and many new languages. When it was announced that we would be a dispersal town, I immediately wrote to the council, giving plenty of information, including names and addresses of churches and Christian organizations who would work together to welcome the asylum seekers in our area.

The council could offer certain facilities but not necessarily the TLC! As a result, two drop-in centres began, where food, advice, games, encouragement and a friendly welcome were offered. Everyone involved embarked on a sharp learning curve. We made many mistakes, but carried on and, we hope, improved our skills in hospitality.

Local believers were very generous with gifts of food, baby clothes, toiletries and so on, but few had the courage to pop in and actually meet any real asylum seekers face to face. When we invited a group of Iraqi men to supper, or two or three Nigerian women, people would say, 'You're so brave having them into your home. What if they…' and their voices trailed off as they imagined our house being stripped of possessions. It is so easy to give a box of food or money. Sometimes that is all we can do, but if we read today's readings thoughtfully and willingly, it may be that Jesus is asking more of us.

....

As Christians, is there any option for us to say, 'I don't do foreigners or drop-outs?' Are we free to wriggle out of obeying Christ's words? Try smiling at someone—a homeless person or a refugee. Next week, say 'Hi'. Let the Lord arrange anything more.

SM

Hospitable silence

When Job's three friends... heard about all the troubles that had come upon him, they set out from their homes and met together by agreement to... comfort him... Then they sat on the ground with him for seven days and seven nights. No one said a word to him, because they saw how great his suffering was.

Job's friends generally get a very bad press: they give so much advice, are so judgmental and are so sure they have something important to say. In spite of that, though, they did exceptionally well to begin with. They visited Job as a trio. In sight of the enormous disaster that had overcome Job, a joint visit gave them courage to support him (v. 11). They were not ashamed to show their emotions (v. 12), and they did not give cheap comfort but held their tongues (v. 13). It must have been very difficult to sit quietly for seven days. It is so easy to chip in with easy reassurance. They waited in sympathetic silence until Job poured out his grief (3:1–26). When at last it was time to say something, how did Eliphaz begin (4:2)?

When I had just come out of hospital after having a mastectomy, I was a bit weepy on occasions, as there is a sense of bereavement about such an operation. A friend rang and quickly told me to pull myself together. 'After all,' she said, 'it's not as if you've had a leg amputated.' Whoops!

After the tsunami disaster, we heard that an asylum seeker staying in our house had lost 24 members of his family in the great wave. How could we possibly respond to him in such a tragedy? We lit a fire, prepared food and invited him in. We waited and listened until, very gradually, he was able to talk in broken sentences. We would have liked him to share more or to weep, but he was in too great a state of steely shock. Words did not come easily; nor were words what he needed.

....

To my shame, I once crossed the road to avoid speaking to a friend whose husband had committed suicide. She later told me that the greatest comfort was a friend who just sat in the room with her. Having read about Job's friends, I hope I would act differently now.

SM

A meal of reconciliation

When they landed, they saw a fire of burning coals there with fish on it, and some bread. Jesus said to them, 'Bring some of the fish you have just caught.' Simon Peter climbed aboard and dragged the net ashore. It was full of large fish... When they had finished eating, Jesus said to Simon Peter, 'Simon son of John, do you love me more than these?' 'Yes, Lord,' he said, 'you know that I love you.' Jesus said, 'Feed my lambs.'

Can you imagine the smell of the fish cooking over the fire and the bread warming on the stones? After a night's fruitless fishing, the disciples must have thought that food had never tasted so good. Not only was it much-needed nourishment; it was also a meal of reconciliation. They were back where they belonged, in fellowship with Jesus. They were no longer the cowardly disciples who had fled from the garden to avoid being present during the crucifixion. Here was Christ welcoming them with warm hospitality. They were his guests.

In your family, are there people who never speak to each other, rifts that are never mentioned or tragedies that have split some people's loyalties? Perhaps you can learn something from Jesus in these verses.

- Jesus made the first move (vv. 4–5).
- Jesus had an appetizing meal ready (v. 9).
- Jesus gave them time to eat and relax (vv. 12–13).
- Only then, after the meal, did Jesus tackle the anguish hanging in the air between him and Peter. He did not rebuke Peter for past failings. Instead he recommissioned him and gave him weighty new tasks (vv. 15–19).

Strains and misunderstandings often happen in family life, but hospitality can avert severe broken relations.

....

Take a five-minute break some time today and read how a quick-thinking woman gained reconciliation with a very angry David (1 Samuel 25:1–35).

SM

The hospitality of outstretched arms

In the same way the chief priests and the teachers of the law mocked him among themselves. 'He saved others,' they said, 'but he can't save himself! Let this Messiah, this king of Israel, come down now from the cross, that we may see and believe.'

What has this reading got to do with hospitality? The story of Christ's death and suffering on our behalf was prepared much earlier than two thousand years ago. Some think it was planned when Adam and Eve's disobedience shattered the purity of life in the garden. But no, it was planned even before that. Read Revelation 13:8 and you will see that since the very creation of the world God had foreseen how we would turn to sin and would need a redeemer.

God's wonderful generosity in his creation, with so much to delight us and so much to discover, which he invited us to share, would be spoiled by us, and he knew it. Even so, his generous compassionate heart cries out to us. He will draw us back. He will save us. That is his deepest hospitality, to invite us again to enjoy his presence.

'For God so loved the world that he gave his one and only Son, that whoever believes in him shall not perish but have eternal life' (John 3:16). The cross is the symbol of the biggest welcome ever offered. Christ's outstretched arms offer us forgiveness, new life and a place of belonging that stretches beyond our imagination.

'For he chose us in him before the creation of the world to be holy and blameless in his sight. In love he predestined us for adoption to sonship through Jesus Christ' (Ephesians 1:4–5). What greater offer of hospitality can there be than to offer us adoption?

Realize afresh that you are loved, chosen, adopted and invited to share in life with this very Creator. What an invitation! But have you actually accepted it?

....

'Perhaps we shrink from receiving fully the loving gift of God because we sense that it will make us images of God and bearers of God's hospitality—and if we look at Jesus on trial, Jesus crucified, we know the cost of that' (Rowan Williams, Christ on Trial, Fount).

SM

One of the skills of hospitality is helping a guest to feel comfortable and at home. Familiarity need not 'breed contempt', as the saying goes. Sometimes familiarity is exactly what's wanted to put someone at ease. When we have guests to stay from different parts of the world, we might turn the heating up if they're from a hot climate, we might serve spicier food if British meals seem too bland or, if a guest has different customs, we go out of our way to accommodate them. For example, Japanese guests are used to showering before soaking in a hot bath. Making the surroundings more familiar helps to put guests at their ease.

God longs to welcome us into our heavenly home, but God is Spirit, so how can we feel at home with him? As the apostle John explained, 'The Word became flesh and made his dwelling among us' (John 1:14, TNIV). God took the initiative and moved towards us. Jesus made it possible for us to become familiar with our awesome Creator God. THE MESSAGE puts it like this: 'The Word became flesh and blood, and moved into the neighbourhood.'

Anne Coomes leads us through the final days of the year, turning our focus to the familiar Christmas story as recorded by Luke. Although the story is probably well known to you, ask God to draw near to you and your loved ones in a special way over the next few days. Make time to focus on Jesus, accepting the invitation into his presence and welcoming him into all you do through the festive season. You might find that the words of this 15th-century hymn are an appropriate prayer:

Come down, O love divine, seek Thou this soul of mine,
And visit it with Thine own ardour glowing.
O Comforter, draw near, within my heart appear,
And kindle it, Thy holy flame bestowing.

O let it freely burn, till earthly passions turn
To dust and ashes in its heat consuming;
And let Thy glorious light shine ever on my sight,
And clothe me round, the while my path illuming.

BIANCO OF SIENA (D. 1434), TRANSLATED FROM ITALIAN TO ENGLISH BY RICHARD F. LITTLEDALE IN 1867.

Why the Christmas story was written

It seemed good also to me to write an orderly account for you, most excellent Theophilus, so that you may know the certainty of the things you have been taught.

Christmas week is upon us. The school nativity plays are over but the Christmas carols go on and the Christmas cards still arrive, reminding us of the angel, the virgin Mary, the baby Jesus and the shepherds. Do you ever wonder where all the details come from and if they are true? If you want to read the Christmas story, there is only one place to go: the Gospel of Luke. Only Luke tells us the story of the birth of the Messiah—how the angel Gabriel visited Mary, how Mary and Joseph went to Bethlehem, how Jesus was born in a manger and then visited by wondering shepherds.

The amazing thing is that Luke was a Gentile. He was the only Gentile to write a Gospel and his is the fullest story of the birth of the Messiah to be found anywhere. So why did Luke feel the need to write this 'orderly account' of events?

For one thing, Luke was in a supreme position to write a Gospel. He was an educated Christian Gentile of some standing in the early Church, who had travelled with Paul and knew Mary and other disciples. So he'd had plenty of time to 'carefully investigate everything from the beginning' (v. 3).

Secondly, the years were passing. By now it was about AD63, and the 'first generation' Christians—the apostles and first disciples—were dying out. How long would their poignant memories last if they were not written down? Christianity is based not on nice ideas but on the historical birth, life and death of Jesus Christ. People needed to know the facts if they were to be confident of their faith in him. Luke's concern for his friend was that 'you may know the certainty of the things you have been taught'.

....

Confidence that Christianity is absolutely trustworthy is what we also need today. Thank God that Luke's Gospel is as relevant for us as it was to Theophilus in the first century.

AC

Your son will be a great success

'Your wife Elizabeth will bear you a son, and you are to call him John. He will be a joy and delight to you, and many will rejoice because of his birth... Many of the people of Israel will he bring back to the Lord their God.'

Why should the gospel of Jesus begin with John the Baptist? It had been about 400 years since God had last spoken to Israel through a prophet. Since then, silence. The old testament, or old covenant between God and humankind, based on the law, was complete.

Four hundred years on, the Roman empire ruled the world, and tiny Israel was a subjugated people with no future. Yet now, at the bleakest of times, the long-promised Messiah was coming at last. The problem was that, after 400 years, Israel was morally asleep, so, to wake the people up, God sent John the Baptist. John's great work would be to give a clarion call to Israel to repent, to prepare themselves for the coming of their Messiah. A new covenant with humankind was about to begin and John was sent ahead as the messenger.

John was born to the most unlikely parents. Zechariah was an elderly priest and his wife Elizabeth was both barren and elderly. In fact, when the angel Gabriel appeared to Zechariah, Zechariah even refused to believe that a son would be born. Yet this son, John, would bring his parents great joy and delight. Why? Because he would wear camel hair and live on locusts and wild honey? Hardly a worldly success! No, John would delight his parents because he would accomplish something extraordinary: he would help to turn Israel back to the Lord.

If you have children, what could they do to bring you joy and delight? Follow a certain career? Make lots of money? Marry the 'right' sort of person? How would you feel if instead they wanted to devote their lives to 'bringing people back to the Lord' in some way? What we want for our children says a lot about the values we hold most dear.

....

Use the words of Proverbs 4 to pray for the children and young people that you know.

AC

The angel Gabriel goes to Mary

In the sixth month of Elizabeth's pregnancy, God sent the angel Gabriel... to a virgin pledged to be married to a man named Joseph... The angel went to her and said, 'Greetings, you who are highly favoured! The Lord is with you.'

Gabriel's visit to the virgin Mary is probably the most famous encounter in the Bible. Gabriel began by honouring Mary, and Mary's reaction is revealing. Instead of being pleased and eagerly excited to know more, she was 'greatly troubled' (v. 29). She was not flattered by upbeat words that she did not see as being true. She knew she was no more than a local teenage girl.

The angel's next words were hardly likely to calm her: 'Do not be afraid, Mary, you have found favour with God. You will conceive and give birth to a son, and you are to call him Jesus.' A baby! This was life-changing news indeed. Mary must have been stunned. 'How will this be, since I am a virgin?' (v. 34). A fair enough question!

Gabriel went on to explain the mystery of the incarnation in a simple line: 'the power of the Most High will overshadow you' (v. 35). There is nothing like this in other religions. Some Greek legends tell of gods mating with women—which is something very different. Only in Christianity do we find the account of a truly virgin conception and birth. The resulting baby would be the 'holy one', the 'Son of God'.

So, in a culture where immorality often resulted in death by stoning, Mary, who was only engaged, was going to produce a baby. The implications for her own safety were frightening. Yet Mary's response to this staggering news was sublimely dignified and simple. Her automatic reaction revealed her heartfelt attitude towards God: 'I am the Lord's servant. May it be to me according to your word' (v. 38). She would trust God to handle all the consequences of his will for her life.

....

None of us will ever be Mary, but each one of us can still say, 'I am the Lord's servant. May it be to me as he has said.' Not according to my ambitions or desires for the future—but according to his will.

AC

129

Elizabeth hears Mary at the door

'Blessed are you among women, and blessed is the child you will bear! ... As soon as the sound of your greeting reached my ears, the baby in my womb leaped for joy. Blessed is she who has believed that the Lord would fulfil his promises to her.'

The angel Gabriel had told Mary that Elizabeth was six months pregnant. Within days, Mary must have hurried to be with Elizabeth in her small hill town in Judah, because Luke tells us that she stayed three months, by which time John's birth was due.

The angel Gabriel had not told Elizabeth about Mary, but he did not need to: as soon as the pregnant Mary walked through the door, the Holy Spirit revealed to the unborn John and his mother just whose presence was now in the house. Elizabeth was ecstatic over the Lord's blessing on young Mary. It is to Elizabeth's great credit that there was not a hint of jealousy that she carried only John, not Jesus.

It was the eve of the two greatest births in history. Elizabeth and Mary had been chosen not for any advantages they naturally possessed: neither was rich, privileged, educated or well-connected. They had been chosen because of their willing spirits: they were both willing to believe and obey God. God can work with such women.

Psalm 32:8 tells us, 'I will instruct you and teach you in the way which you shall go.' Psalm 138:8 gives us the assurance, 'The Lord will fulfil his purpose for me' (NIV). Proverbs 3:6 urges us, 'Acknowledge him, and he will direct your paths.' Isaiah 30:21 says, 'Your ears will hear a voice... "This is the way, walk in it"' (TNIV).

So God, in revealing his will to Mary and Elizabeth, was not acting in a unique way. He has a will for each and every one of us. All we need is what Mary and Elizabeth both demonstrated: a listening ear and a willing heart. Praise God! It's exciting, isn't it, to think that the Creator of the universe wants to guide you into finding his plans for *you*?

....

Read Ephesians 1:3–14 to see how detailed God's plans are for you. Then respond to God's goodness with your own prayer of praise.

AC

The Magnificat

'My soul glorifies the Lord and my spirit rejoices in God my Saviour, for he has been mindful of the humble state of his servant.'

Mary's magnificent hymn of thanksgiving to God, the Magnificat, gets its name from its first word in the Latin Vulgate translation. Mary's words have been used in the praises of the Christian Church from earliest times.

The idea that Mary should burst forth with it now, in her meeting with Elizabeth rather than her meeting with Gabriel, has puzzled some male Bible scholars, but that is because they don't understand women. Mary had been awed by Gabriel's appearance and news of Jesus' impending birth: she felt too self-conscious to start exulting with an archangel.

Like any young woman, Mary would have wanted a close girl-friend to confide in. Perhaps, though, Gabriel understood her better than she realized, because it was he who hinted that she might want to visit Elizabeth. So off Mary goes, and by the time she reaches Elizabeth she is bursting with thankfulness and joy. When she walks through the door to discover that Elizabeth already has an inkling of what has happened and is delighted for her—well, Mary can contain herself no longer. No woman could.

Since childhood, Mary would have been steeped in the language of the Old Testament. She has just been told that she is going to bear the Messiah, so it is no surprise that her thoughts would have gone back to Hannah, exulting over the birth of her dearly wanted son, Samuel. It's no wonder that Mary's wonderful song of thanksgiving takes a form similar to that of Hannah, no wonder that it is almost wholly made up of Old Testament quotations. Mary directs her love and praise to God the Father, who has acted throughout the history of her people and is now acting again, through her young life.

Except for the second part of verse 48, any one of us could sing the Magnificat, for the focus is on what God has done for his people, not how special any one of us is. Today, why not use it as your own song of worship to the Lord?

AC

131

The birth of John the Baptist

'And you, my child, will be called a prophet of the Most High; for you will go on before the Lord to prepare the way for him.

In due course, Elizabeth gave birth to her son. The relatives were about to name him Zechariah but Elizabeth and Zechariah were adamant: his name was John. When Gabriel had first come to him more than nine months before, Zechariah, the trained priest, had doubted the archangel. He had failed to believe God, whereas Mary, an illiterate young girl, passed with flying colours. 'Professional' religious knowledge is not everything. By now, however, even Zechariah had got the message and his act of obedience in giving the name John was immediately blessed by God: 'his mouth was opened... and he began to speak, praising God' (v. 64).

Zechariah's great hymn of praise is called the Benedictus, from its opening word in Latin. In a way, it is the first ever Christmas carol, because it is the first recorded song we have that sings of the coming of the Christ-child, the Messiah. Some scholars have considered the Benedictus as the last prophecy of the old covenant and the first prophecy of the new covenant. After centuries of waiting, the Messiah was on the way and Zechariah's son would be his herald. Zechariah would have been overwhelmed by this realization. There had been no prophet in Israel for four centuries. John would not be able to save people, but he would point them towards a man who could.

Any parent is proud when their child begins to flourish and find a role in life, but ahead of Elizabeth and Zechariah there lay tragedy. When John was arrested, imprisoned and then beheaded, it is not hard to imagine their grief. If they were still alive, they could only stand firm and paraphrase Mary's words of so many years before: 'Let it be to him according to your will.' They knew for sure that John had not lived his life in vain: he had accomplished what he had been born to do.

....

When disaster hits our children, it is devastating. Then, all we can do is commit them to God and his overriding care. Psalm 147:3 is a sure promise of his love for us, even in times of tragedy.

AC

The birth of Jesus Christ

In those days Caesar Augustus issued a decree that a census should
be taken… So Joseph also went up… to Bethlehem the town of
David… and [Mary] gave birth to her firstborn, a son. She wrapped
him in cloths and placed him in a manger, because there was no room
for them in the inn.

Here is a curious thing: for millions of people in this country, the story
of Jesus' birth is practically all they know about the Christian faith. And
yet, in the entire Bible, that birth is covered only by Luke, and in a
mere seven verses. Luke begins by setting Jesus' birth against the backdrop of the wider events of the time. Caesar Augustus, whose rule as
absolute monarch from 30BC to AD14 at least provided a period of outward calm (later helpful to the spread of Christianity), had decreed that
a census should be taken of the entire Roman world. Imagine attempting that without a computer!

Since Joseph was of the family of David, he had to report to
Bethlehem. He took Mary, still only his 'betrothed', with him. He
shared her secret about the pregnancy and would have wanted to protect her from any harm. When they reached Bethlehem, Mary went
into labour. There was no room for them in the inn, so they took shelter with the animals. It might have been in a stable, or even, as the
early Church Father Justin Martyr tells us, in a local cave. Certainly,
about AD330, Constantine the Great built a church over a cave and the
current church on the site has been there for about 1600 years.

Mary had no help with the birth, for she herself had to wrap Jesus in
the 'swaddling cloths' that were the custom of the time. As to the exact
date of his birth, no one knows. It may be that the early Christians chose
25 December to supplant the pagan Mithras birth-feast. Whatever the
reason, this date was first celebrated in Rome in 354, in Constantinople
in 379, and in Antioch in 388.

....

*Does your faith ever falter when you go from the heights of a spiri-
tual experience to the troubles of everyday life? Think of Mary. She
had angels to announce her pregnancy and the birth, but no help
or even decent shelter when actually giving birth to the Messiah.*

AC

Shepherds and angels

And there were shepherds living out in the fields near by, keeping watch over their flocks at night. An angel of the Lord appeared to them, and the glory of the Lord shone around them… 'Do not be afraid. I bring you good news of great joy that will be for all the people.'

Luke's story of the shepherds and the angels is so well known that it seems to come right off the front of a Christmas card—happy angels calling down to bewildered shepherds.

The shepherds in New Testament times lived with their flocks day and night. It was a tough, dirty life and, because of this, they were seen as ceremonially unclean and unfit to approach the temple for worship. Shepherds were close to the bottom of the social scale, avoided by polite society. Yet it was the shepherds to whom God first revealed the amazing news: the Messiah had come! For those simple men, stretched out on the ground with their flocks, the heavens literally opened up that night. One minute they were looking up at the stars, the next minute the sky was full of angelic beings and the glory of God.

There is but a thin veil separating us from the unseen realm of the kingdom of the heavens. It is too easy to think of heaven as a faraway place, remote from us 'down here' on tangible earth. But the New Testament speaks of, literally, the kingdom of the heavens, of the sky and air all around us. If we could but see, there are angels all around us and spiritual forces of darkness as well.

For the shepherds, the veil was pulled back that night. We can only imagine their joy and amazement, yet the pattern of God's grace reaching out towards them first—and their faith in grateful response— is the way God acts in our lives, as well. It was only after the shepherds saw the glory of God that they could respond to God in faith and in obedience, by seeking the Saviour. We can, too.

....

How did God first take the initiative in reaching out to you? Can you recall what your life was like before you had faith in him?

AC

The Nunc Dimittis

'You may now dismiss your servant in peace. For my eyes have seen your salvation, which you have prepared in the sight of all nations: a light for revelation to the Gentiles, and the glory of your people Israel.'

A woman was considered ceremonially impure for 40 days after the birth of a son. After that time, Joseph and Mary took Jesus to the temple in nearby Jerusalem. Jewish law required that they consecrate their firstborn male to the Lord. Well-off people would include a lamb in their 'purification sacrifices', so it seems Joseph and Mary were poor—they could afford only a pair of doves or two young pigeons.

Their trip to the temple was peaceful, so scholars believe that the wise men had not yet arrived in Jerusalem, talking of a star and a new king and thus stirring Herod to the mass murder of all young Jewish males. Instead their visit was full of hope and promise, for Joseph and Mary encountered two temple people who, to their amazement, immediately saw greatness in their tiny infant.

Simeon and Anna were both devout Jews who had spent their lives longing for the 'consolation of Israel' (v. 25), but, what is more, they were prophets. After hundreds of years of Old Testament prophets looking forward to the Messiah, it was given to Simeon and Anna to be the prophets who actually met him and recognized him for who he was. It was the crowning moment of their lives—so much so that Simeon declared himself now ready to die.

In his magnificent Nunc Dimittis (again, so named after its opening words in Latin), Simeon says an astonishing thing about this tiny Messiah. The Jews had always expected the Messiah to be *their* Messiah, but Simeon declares that the Messiah will be for *all* people: 'a light for revelation to the Gentiles, and the glory of your people Israel' (v. 32). This was unheard of—the God of the Jews offering salvation to all humankind!

....

Spend some time praising God for sending Jesus and for including you in his salvation plan.

AC

When Jesus visited the temple

'Why were you searching for me?' he asked. 'Didn't you know I had to be in my Father's house?' ... And Jesus grew in wisdom and stature, and in favour with God and people.

The only story we have of Jesus as a boy is found here in Luke's Gospel. Again, it takes place in the temple. All Jewish men (though not necessarily women) were expected to attend the temple three times a year, at the festivals of Passover, Pentecost and Tabernacles. Not everyone made it each time: travel was difficult and dangerous. It was Joseph and Mary's custom to go up at Passover, the feast that commemorated the deliverance of the nation from Egypt.

On this occasion, trouble began on the way home. In these walking 'caravans' of people, it was usual for women and small children to go on ahead, while the men followed with the bigger boys. It could well be that Joseph and Mary each thought Jesus was with the other. They were frantic when they realized he was missing.

They finally found him back in Jerusalem, among the teachers in the temple precincts, listening and asking questions and amazing the teachers with his insights. When his parents reproached him, Jesus seems to have been surprised. He utters here his first ever recorded words (the verses printed above). Luke must have thought this well worth remembering—that even as a boy Jesus recognized his unique relationship to God. Joseph and Mary, meanwhile, were learning what it meant, bit by bit.

It is well known that young people can have an immense awareness of God. Being young is no bar to an intense desire for spirituality. Those who are parents can help nurture this awareness through praying and reading the Bible with them. (Sometimes a children's version is easiest, for starters). This will help them as they themselves prepare to fulfil the unique life that God has given them.

....

Pray for your friends' and relatives' children by name.

Proverbs 22:6 encourages us to do everything we can for our children.

AC

John the Baptist gets busy

The word of God came to John son of Zechariah in the wilderness. He went into all the country around the Jordan, preaching a baptism of repentance for the forgiveness of sins.

John was the prophet who bridged the Old and New Testaments. His role was to make the way ready for the beginning of Jesus' public ministry. When the word of God came to him, John obeyed. What he proclaimed then to the Jews of the first century is as true for us today.

First of all, John called on the people to repent. This was not a request to feel some regret for their past misdeeds. It was a clarion call to stop and turn, to forsake a life of self and sin for a life of obedience to God. Secondly, John was scathing about mere religious ritual as a way of pleasing God. Sadly, even today there are many who rely on church rituals to give them merit with God. Thirdly, John told his listeners to put their money where their mouth was. Genuine repentance, he said, must bear the fruit of action. It meant caring for others in practical and sacrificial ways, giving clothing to those in need and being honest in one's dealings (vv. 11–14). He did not tell the tax collectors and soldiers to change their jobs, but to do them with integrity.

Have you ever noticed how the Bible links evidence of true repentance with the financial side of life? Jesus said more about money than he said about heaven and hell combined. Money must be managed or it will manage us (Matthew 6:24), so it appears that our wallets are on the cutting edge of repentance and true conversion. Jesus said that his true followers will feed the hungry, clothe the naked and so on.

John's was a baptism of repentance, but Jesus' would be a baptism of regeneration, of remaking us through the power of the Spirit. Repentance turns us towards Jesus, and then Jesus, by his Spirit in us, enables us to be different people.

....

John the Baptist was called to point the way for others to meet Jesus. We too are called to be trailblazers, introducers and bridge builders, but, like John, we need the power of the Holy Spirit in our lives.

AC

Contributors

Anita Cleverly is passionate about passing on biblical literacy to the next generation. She and her husband led a French-speaking church in Paris until September 2002, when they moved to St Aldate's, Oxford.

Fiona Barnard is a staff member of Friends International. Her principal work is among international students, encouraging local Christians to reach out in friendship to those temporarily far from home.

Rosemary Green recently spent two years in the USA, working in pastoral ministry in a new Anglican church. 'Retirement' means being an active layperson in her local church and being available to help with 14 (mostly young) grandchildren.

Alie Stibbe works as a Student Administrator at West Herts College. She is also a freelance writer, small-time company director, allotment holder, vicar's wife, mother of four, and a recent graduate.

Christine Platt spent ten years with The Navigators in West Africa, involved in evangelism and discipleship. She now enjoys working as a freelance writer and serving as an elder in her church in New Zealand.

Jennifer Rees Larcombe has six children, all married, and loves playing with her numerous grandchildren. She runs Beauty from Ashes, an organization that helps to support people adjusting to bereavement and trauma.

Chris Leonard lives in Surrey with her husband; both 20 something offspring have fled the nest. With 17 books published, Chris leads many creative writing holidays and workshops. See www.chris-leonard-writing.co.uk

Sylvia Mandeville's work has included teaching and writing books and poetry. She is a Lay Reader in Wales, is learning Welsh and is involved with asylum seekers. Her passion is visiting and praying for Uzbekistan.

Anne Coomes edits a resource website for church magazine editors: parishpump.co.uk. She is also editor of the inhouse magazines for the Billy Graham Evangelistic Association (UK) and Samaritan's Purse (UK).

Other Christina Press titles

Life Path Luci Shaw (£5.99)

Keeping a journal can enrich life as we live it, and bring it all back later. Luci Shaw shows how a journal can also help us grow in our walk with God.

Precious to God Sarah Bowen (£5.99)

Two young people have their expectations shattered by the birth of a handicapped child. What was initially a tragedy is, through faith, transformed into a story of inspiration, hope and spiritual enrichment.

Women Celebrating Faith Ed. Lucinda McDowell (£5.99)

A challenging collection of writings by women from all walks of life, taking time to look back on their lives at forty. No matter what age the reader is, they will be encouraged by the experiences of these women.

Other BRF titles

Play and Pray through Advent Ed. Kay Warrington (£11.99)

This book encourages children and families to participate in the events surrounding the birth of Jesus. It suggests ways in which children can engage creatively with the story, using simple visual items to bring the story to life. The material also includes ideas for crafts and songs.

Growing Women Leaders Rosie Ward (£8.99) *(available Oct 08)*

Surveying the latest scholarship on key scripture passages relating to women leaders, and offering practical advice on growing women leaders today, this book is written to inspire and nurture women already in leadership and to encourage those exploring a call to this ministry.

Quiet Spaces: Noon Ed. Naomi Starkey (£4.99)

The idea of 'noon' contains two contradictory images: the highpoint of the day to which the morning's activity leads, and the time when heat is most intense and a midday rest is needed. Both these images are explored here: 'seizing the day' and also pausing to take stock.

Christina Press Publications Order Form

All of these publications are available from Christian bookshops everywhere or, in case of difficulty, direct from the publisher. Please make your selection below, complete the payment details and send your order with payment as appropriate to:

Christina Press Ltd, 17 Church Road, Tunbridge Wells, Kent TN1 1LG

		Qty	Price	Total
8700	God's Catalyst	___	£8.99	___
8701	Women Celebrating Faith	___	£5.99	___
8702	Precious to God	___	£5.99	___
8703	Angels Keep Watch	___	£5.99	___
8704	Life Path	___	£5.99	___
8705	Pathway Through Grief	___	£6.99	___
8706	Who'd Plant a Church?	___	£5.99	___
8707	Dear God, It's Me and It's Urgent	___	£6.99	___
8708	Not a Super-Saint	___	£6.99	___
8709	The Addiction of a Busy Life	___	£5.99	___
8710	In His Time	___	£5.99	___

POSTAGE AND PACKING CHARGES	UK	Europe	Surface	Air Mail
£7.00 & under	£1.25	£3.00	£3.50	£5.50
£7.10–£29.99	£2.25	£5.50	£6.50	£10.00
£30.00 & over	free	prices on request		

Total cost of books £ ___
Postage and Packing £ ___
TOTAL £ ___

All prices are correct at time of going to press, are subject to the prevailing rate of VAT and may be subject to change without prior warning.

Name _____

Address _____

_____

_____ Postcode _____

Total enclosed £ _____ (cheques should be made payable to 'Christina Press Ltd')

☐ Please do not send me further information about Christina Press publications

BRF Publications Order Form

All of these publications are available from Christian bookshops everywhere, or in case of difficulty direct from the publisher. Please make your selection below, complete the payment details and send your order with payment as appropriate to:

BRF, 15 The Chambers, Vineyard, Abingdon, Oxon OX14 3FE

		Qty	Price	Total
567 5	Play and Pray through Advent	_____	£11.99	_____
575 0	Growing Women Leaders	_____	£8.99	_____
500 2	Quiet Spaces: Fire	_____	£4.99	_____
540 8	Quiet Spaces: Morning	_____	£4.99	_____
541 5	Quiet Spaces: Noon	_____	£4.99	_____

POSTAGE AND PACKING CHARGES				
	UK	Europe	Surface	Air Mail
£7.00 & under	£1.25	£3.00	£3.50	£5.50
£7.10–£29.99	£2.25	£5.50	£6.50	£10.00
£30.00 & over	free	prices on request		

Total cost of books £ _____
Postage and Packing £ _____
TOTAL £ _____

All prices are correct at time of going to press, are subject to the prevailing rate of VAT and may be subject to change without prior warning.

Name _____

Address _____

_____ Postcode _____

Total enclosed £ _____ (cheques should be made payable to 'BRF')
Payment by: cheque ❑ postal order ❑ Visa ❑ Mastercard ❑ Switch ❑

Card no. ❑❑❑❑ ❑❑❑❑ ❑❑❑❑ ❑❑❑❑ ❑❑❑❑

Expires ❑❑❑❑ Security code ❑❑❑ Issue no (Switch) ❑❑❑❑

Signature _____
(essential if paying by credit/Switch card)

❑ Please do not send me further information about BRF publications

Visit the BRF website at www.brf.org.uk

DBDWG0308

BRF is a Registered Charity

Subscription Information

Each issue of *Day by Day with God* is available from Christian book-shops everywhere. Copies may also be available through your church Book Agent or from the person who distributes Bible reading notes in your church.

Alternatively you may obtain *Day by Day with God* on subscription direct from the publishers. There are two kinds of subscription:

Individual Subscriptions are for four copies or less, and include postage and packing. To order an annual Individual Subscription please complete the details on page 144 and send the coupon with payment to BRF in Abingdon. You can also use the form to order a Gift Subscription for a friend.

Church Subscriptions are for five copies or more, sent to one address, and are supplied post free. Church Subscriptions run from 1 May to 30 April each year and are invoiced annually. To order a Church Subscription please complete the details opposite and send the coupon to BRF in Abingdon. You will receive an invoice with the first issue of notes.

All subscription enquiries should be directed to:

BRF
15 The Chambers
Vineyard
Abingdon
Oxon
OX14 3FE

Tel: 01865 319700
Fax: 01865 319701
E-mail: subscriptions@brf.org.uk

Church Subscriptions

The Church Subscription rate for *Day by Day with God* will be £11.25 per person until April 2009.

❏ I would like to take out a church subscription for _____ (Qty) copies.

❏ Please start my order with the January / May / September 2009* issue. I would like to pay annually/receive an invoice with each edition of the notes*.
(*Please delete as appropriate)

Please do not send any money with your order. Send your order to BRF and we will send you an invoice. The Church Subscription year is from May to April. If you start subscribing in the middle of a subscription year we will invoice you for the remaining number of issues left in that year.

Name and address of the person organising the Church Subscription:

Name _____

Address _____

_____

_____

Postcode _____Telephone _____

Church _____

Name of Minister _____

Name and address of the person paying the invoice if the invoice needs to be sent directly to them:

Name _____

Address _____

_____

Postcode _____Telephone _____

Please send your coupon to:

BRF
15 The Chambers
Vineyard
Abingdon
Oxon
OX14 3FE

❏ Please do not send me further information about BRF publications

BRF is a Registered Charity

Individual Subscriptions

❏ I would like to give a gift subscription (please complete both name and address sections below)

❏ I would like to take out a subscription myself (complete your name and address details only once)

Your name _____

Your address _____

_____ Postcode _____

Gift subscription name _____

Gift subscription address _____

_____ Postcode _____

Please send *Day by Day with God* for one year, beginning with the January / May / September 2009 issue: (delete as applicable)

	UK	Surface	Air Mail
Day by Day with God	❏ £13.80	❏ £15.00	❏ £17.10
2-year subscription	❏ £22.50	N/A	N/A

I would like to take out an annual subscription to *Quiet Spaces* beginning with the next available issue:

	UK	Surface	Air Mail
Quiet Spaces	❏ £16.95	❏ £18.45	❏ £20.85

Please complete the payment details below and send your coupon, with appropriate payment, to BRF, 15 The Chambers, Vineyard, Abingdon, Oxon OX14 3FE

Total enclosed £ _____ (cheques should be made payable to 'BRF')
Payment by: cheque ❏ postal order ❏ Visa ❏ Mastercard ❏ Switch ❏

Card no. ☐☐☐☐ ☐☐☐☐ ☐☐☐☐ ☐☐☐☐ ☐☐☐☐ ☐☐

Expires ☐☐☐☐   Security code ☐☐☐   Issue no (Switch) ☐☐☐

Signature _____
(essential if paying by credit/Switch card)

NB: These notes are also available from Christian bookshops everywhere.

❏ Please do not send me further information about BRF publications

DBDWG0308   BRF is a Registered Charity